T0308477

# SIMPLE

# SIMPLE

13-Digit ISBN: 978-1-60433-983-3

10-Digit ISBN: 1-60433-983-7

This book may be ordered by mail from the publisher. Please include $5.99 for postage and handling. Please support your local bookseller first!

Books published by Cider Mill Press Book Publishers are available at special discounts for bulk purchases in the United States by corporations, institutions, and other organizations. For more information, please contact the publisher.

Cider Mill Press Book Publishers

"Where good books are ready for press"

PO Box 454

12 Spring Street

Kennebunkport, Maine 04046

Visit us online!

www.cidermillpress.com

Typography: Black Jack, Garamond, Gotham
Front Cover Image: Spaghetti with Zucchini & Pesto, see page 52
Back Cover Image: Dutch Apple Baby, see page 238
Front Endpaper Image: Pork Loin with Dried Cranberry Sauce, see page 38
Back Endpaper Image: Cherry Clafoutis, see page 230
Image Credits: Photos on pages 17, 18, 40, 44, 80, 87, 88, 94, 98, 101, 106, 110, 113, 114, 117, 118, 121, 122, 126, 129, 132, 136, 139, 143, 147, 148, 151, 152, 156, 161, 162, 177, 178, 181, 192, 195, 196, 200, 203, 204, 212, and 236 courtesy of Cider Mill Press Book Publishers.

All other photos used under official license from Shutterstock.

Printed in China

3 4 5 6 7 8 9 0

# SIMPLE

*Over 100 Classic Recipes for the
Easiest and Quickest Way to Cook*

CIDER MILL PRESS

BOOK
PUBLISHERS
KENNEBUNKPORT, MAINE

# TABLE *of* CONTENTS

✳ ✳ ✳

INTRODUCTION · 7

*Chapter 1:* SIMPLE STAPLES · 11

*Chapter 2:* IN A FLASH · 35

*Chapter 3:* LOW AND SLOW · 93

*Chapter 4:* IN THE OVEN · 131

*Chapter 5:* MARINATE ON THAT · 159

*Chapter 6:* WHAT'S LEFT · 185

*Chapter 7:* SWEET CRAVINGS · 215

*Index* · 248

# INTRODUCTION

❋ ❋ ❋

We all want to simplify our lives, to free up more time and clear our heads. But it can be hard to know exactly how one goes about achieving these goals. Is it best to focus on actions that are quickly and easily accomplished? Should you involve yourself in processes that rely on long spans of time rather than your energy and attention? Or is the answer to intelligently employ the energy of outside elements to ensure that yours doesn't get used up?

The answer, as usual, can be found in the kitchen. As it is at the center of so much of the time and thought we devote to everyday involvements, trimming away excess and employing proper techniques in your cooking are of the utmost importance if one wants to get a handle on their free time, and life.

The kitchen is also a place where the value of a perspective that prioritizes simplicity becomes readily apparent. Whether it is a steak quickly seared in a cast-iron skillet, a brisket that spends all afternoon in a slow cooker acquiring unsurpassed flavor and texture, or a flank steak that slowly makes its way toward mouthwatering while steeping in a carne asada marinade, cutting through complication when the time comes to prepare a meal is not just a way to set your life in order, it's also the best way to lift your cooking to another level.

# CHAPTER 1

# SIMPLE
# STAPLES

---

*Part of simplifying matters in the kitchen is making sure you always have a few standbys—stocks, sauces, and condiments—at your fingertips. If you have quality chicken stock (see page 12) or marinara sauce (see page 31) on hand, you're already halfway to a high-quality meal, assuming you've made them at home and aren't relying on store-bought varieties. With that in mind, we've gathered those essential recipes that put you a step ahead.*

# Chicken Stock

YIELD: **8 CUPS**

ACTIVE TIME: **20 MINUTES**

TOTAL TIME: **6 HOURS**

*A must for any homemade soup, this stock is also great when you need to deglaze a pan.*

## INGREDIENTS

7 LBS. CHICKEN BONES, RINSED

4 CUPS CHOPPED YELLOW ONIONS

2 CUPS CHOPPED CARROTS

2 CUPS CHOPPED CELERY

3 GARLIC CLOVES, CRUSHED

3 SPRIGS FRESH THYME

1 TEASPOON BLACK PEPPERCORNS

1 BAY LEAF

## DIRECTIONS

1. Place the chicken bones in a stockpot and cover with cold water. Bring to a simmer over medium-high heat and use a ladle to skim off any impurities that rise to the surface. Add the vegetables, thyme, peppercorns, and bay leaf, reduce the heat to low, and simmer for 5 hours, while skimming to remove any impurities that rise to the surface.

2. Strain, allow to cool slightly, and transfer to the refrigerator. Leave uncovered and allow to cool completely. Remove layer of fat and cover. The stock will keep in the refrigerator for 3 to 5 days, and in the freezer for up to 3 months.

# Beef Stock

YIELD: **8 CUPS**

ACTIVE TIME: **20 MINUTES**

TOTAL TIME: **6 HOURS**

*If you want an extra-smooth stock, try using veal bones instead of beef bones.*

## INGREDIENTS

7 LBS. BEEF BONES, RINSED

4 CUPS CHOPPED YELLOW ONIONS

2 CUPS CHOPPED CARROTS

2 CUPS CHOPPED CELERY

3 GARLIC CLOVES, CRUSHED

3 SPRIGS FRESH THYME

1 TEASPOON BLACK PEPPERCORNS

1 BAY LEAF

## DIRECTIONS

1. Place the beef bones in a stockpot and cover with cold water. Bring to a simmer over medium-high heat and use a ladle to skim off any impurities that rise to the surface. Add the vegetables, thyme, peppercorns, and bay leaf, reduce the heat to low, and simmer for 5 hours, while skimming to remove any impurities that rise to the surface.

2. Strain, allow to cool slightly, and transfer to the refrigerator. Leave uncovered and allow to cool completely. Remove the layer of fat and cover. The stock will keep in the refrigerator for 3 to 5 days, and in the freezer for up to 3 months.

# Fish Stock

YIELD: **6 CUPS**

ACTIVE TIME: **20 MINUTES**

TOTAL TIME: **4 HOURS**

*Using whitefish will make for the most versatile stock. But if you're making a dish that features salmon, feel free to substitute salmon bones and heads.*

## INGREDIENTS

¼ CUP OLIVE OIL

1 LEEK, TRIMMED, RINSED WELL, AND CHOPPED

1 LARGE YELLOW ONION, UNPEELED, ROOT CLEANED, CHOPPED

2 LARGE CARROTS, CHOPPED

1 CELERY STALK, CHOPPED

¾ LB. WHITEFISH BODIES

4 SPRIGS FRESH PARSLEY

3 SPRIGS FRESH THYME

2 BAY LEAVES

1 TEASPOON BLACK PEPPERCORNS

1 TEASPOON KOSHER SALT

8 CUPS WATER

## DIRECTIONS

1. Place the olive oil in a stockpot and warm over low heat. Add the vegetables and cook until the liquid they release has evaporated. Add the whitefish bodies, the aromatics, the salt, and the water to the pot, raise the heat to high, and bring to a boil. Reduce heat so that the stock simmers and cook for 3 hours, while skimming to remove any impurities that rise to the surface.

2. Strain the stock through a fine sieve, let it cool slightly, and place in the refrigerator, uncovered, to chill. When the stock is completely cool, remove the fat layer from the top and cover. The stock will keep in the refrigerator for 3 to 5 days, and in the freezer for up to 3 months.

# Vegetable Stock

YIELD: **6 CUPS**

ACTIVE TIME: **20 MINUTES**

TOTAL TIME: **3 HOURS**

*A great way to make use of your vegetable trimmings. Just avoid starchy vegetables such as potatoes, as they will make the stock cloudy.*

## INGREDIENTS

2 TABLESPOONS OLIVE OIL

2 LARGE LEEKS, TRIMMED AND RINSED WELL

2 LARGE CARROTS, PEELED AND SLICED

2 CELERY STALKS, SLICED

2 LARGE YELLOW ONIONS, SLICED

3 GARLIC CLOVES, UNPEELED BUT SMASHED

2 SPRIGS FRESH PARSLEY

2 SPRIGS FRESH THYME

1 BAY LEAF

8 CUPS WATER

½ TEASPOON BLACK PEPPERCORNS

SALT, TO TASTE

## DIRECTIONS

1. Place the olive oil and the vegetables in a large stockpot and cook over low heat until the liquid the vegetables release has evaporated. This will allow the flavor of the vegetables to become concentrated.

2. Add the parsley, thyme, bay leaf, water, peppercorns, and salt. Raise the heat to high and bring to a boil. Reduce heat so that the stock simmers and cook for 2 hours, while skimming to remove any impurities that rise to the surface.

3. Strain the stock through a fine sieve, let it cool slightly, and place in the refrigerator, uncovered, to chill. Remove the fat layer and cover. The stock will keep in the refrigerator for 3 to 5 days, and in the freezer for up to 3 months.

# Blender Hollandaise

YIELD: **1 CUP**

ACTIVE TIME: **5 MINUTES**

TOTAL TIME: **5 MINUTES**

*The blender puts this beloved, buttery sauce instantly within reach. It is perfect over roasted asparagus and other vegetables.*

## INGREDIENTS

3 LARGE EGG YOLKS

¼ TEASPOON KOSHER SALT

2 TABLESPOONS FRESH LEMON JUICE

1 STICK UNSALTED BUTTER

## DIRECTIONS

1. Place the egg yolks, salt, and lemon juice in a blender and blitz on high for a few seconds.

2. Melt the butter in a small saucepan over medium-low heat, being careful not to let it brown.

3. While the butter is still hot, turn on the blender and, with the top off, slowly drizzle the hot butter into the egg mixture until fully emulsified. Taste, adjust seasoning if necessary, and use immediately.

# Roasted Tomato Salsa

YIELD: **1 CUP**

ACTIVE TIME: **20 MINUTES**

TOTAL TIME: **2 HOURS**

*Roasting the tomatoes brings out their sweet side and makes this salsa good enough to enjoy on its own.*

## INGREDIENTS

1 LB. RIPE TOMATOES, CORED AND HALVED

½ TABLESPOON OLIVE OIL

SALT AND PEPPER, TO TASTE

2 TABLESPOONS MINCED YELLOW ONION

½ JALAPEÑO PEPPER, STEMMED, SEEDED, AND MINCED

1 TABLESPOON FINELY CHOPPED FRESH CILANTRO

1 TABLESPOON FRESH LIME JUICE

## DIRECTIONS

1. Preheat your oven to 450°F. Place the tomatoes, olive oil, salt, and pepper in a large bowl and toss to coat. Let stand for 30 minutes.

2. Place the tomatoes, cut-side down, on a baking sheet, place them in the oven, and roast until they start to char and soften, about 10 minutes. Carefully turn the tomatoes over and roast until they start bubbling, about 5 minutes. Remove from the oven and let the tomatoes cool completely.

3. Chop the tomatoes and place them in a bowl with the remaining ingredients. Stir to combine and let stand at room temperature for 45 minutes. Taste, adjust seasoning if necessary, and serve. The salsa will keep in the refrigerator for up to 2 days.

# Salsa Verde

YIELD: **1 CUP**

ACTIVE TIME: **5 MINUTES**

TOTAL TIME: **15 MINUTES**

*The tart and sweet tomatillo is one of the easiest and most delicious ways to add a burst of color to your table.*

## INGREDIENTS

6 TOMATILLOS, HUSKED AND RINSED

8 SERRANO PEPPERS, STEMMED AND SEEDED TO TASTE

½ YELLOW ONION

2 GARLIC CLOVES, MINCED

SALT, TO TASTE

¼ CUP OLIVE OIL

FRESH CILANTRO, FINELY CHOPPED, FOR GARNISH

## DIRECTIONS

1. Place the tomatillos and serrano peppers in a large saucepan and cover with water. Bring to a boil and cook until the tomatillos start to lose their bright green color, about 10 minutes.

2. Drain and transfer the tomatillos and peppers to a blender. Add all of the remaining ingredients, except for the cilantro, and puree until smooth. Top with the cilantro and serve. The salsa will keep in the refrigerator for up to 2 days.

# Guacamole

YIELD: **2 CUPS**

ACTIVE TIME: **5 MINUTES**

TOTAL TIME: **5 MINUTES**

*Wholly suitable as a side or as the centerpiece of a friendly gathering.*

## INGREDIENTS

2 TABLESPOONS MINCED
RED ONION

ZEST AND JUICE OF 1 LIME

SALT, TO TASTE

1 JALAPEÑO PEPPER, STEMMED,
SEEDED, AND MINCED

FLESH FROM 3 AVOCADOS,
CHOPPED

2 TABLESPOONS CHOPPED
FRESH CILANTRO

1 PLUM TOMATO, CONCASSE
(SEE SIDEBAR)

## DIRECTIONS

1. Place the onion, lime zest and juice, salt, and jalapeño in a mixing bowl and stir to combine.

2. Add the avocados and work the mixture with a fork until the desired consistency has been reached. Add the cilantro and tomato, stir to incorporate, and taste. Adjust seasoning if needed and serve immediately.

---

### TOMATO CONCASSE

Concasse, French for "to crush or grind," refers to tomatoes that have been peeled, seeded, and then chopped. To do this easily, boil enough water for a tomato to be submerged and add a pinch of salt. Prepare an ice water bath and score the top of the tomato with a paring knife. Place the tomato in the boiling water for 30 seconds, carefully remove it, and place it in the ice bath. Once the tomato is cool, remove from the water and peel with the paring knife. Cut into quarters, remove the seeds, and chop.

# Basil Pesto

YIELD: **1 CUP**

ACTIVE TIME: **10 MINUTES**

TOTAL TIME: **25 MINUTES**

*This simple pesto is always great to have on hand, as it will give you options in a number of preparations.*

## INGREDIENTS

¼ CUP WALNUTS

3 GARLIC CLOVES

SALT AND PEPPER, TO TASTE

2 CUPS FIRMLY PACKED BASIL LEAVES

½ CUP OLIVE OIL

¼ CUP GRATED PARMESAN CHEESE

¼ CUP GRATED PECORINO SARDO CHEESE

## DIRECTIONS

1. Warm a small skillet over low heat for 1 minute. Add the walnuts and cook, while stirring, until they begin to give off a toasty fragrance, 2 to 3 minutes. Transfer to a plate and let cool completely.

2. Place the garlic, salt, and walnuts in a food processor or blender and pulse until the mixture is a coarse meal. Add the basil and pulse until minced. Transfer the mixture to a mixing bowl and add the oil in a thin stream, whisking constantly to incorporate it.

3. Add the cheeses and stir until thoroughly incorporated. The pesto will keep in the refrigerator for up to 4 days and in the freezer for up to 3 months.

# Marinara Sauce

YIELD: **8 CUPS**

ACTIVE TIME: **20 MINUTES**

TOTAL TIME: **2 HOURS**

*Every great cook needs a foolproof marinara sauce, as there remains no better method to capture the flavor of fresh tomatoes.*

## INGREDIENTS

4 LBS. TOMATOES, QUARTERED

1 LARGE YELLOW ONION, SLICED

15 GARLIC CLOVES, CRUSHED

2 TEASPOONS FINELY CHOPPED FRESH THYME

2 TEASPOONS FINELY CHOPPED FRESH OREGANO

2 TABLESPOONS OLIVE OIL

1½ TABLESPOONS KOSHER SALT

1 TEASPOON BLACK PEPPER

2 TABLESPOONS FINELY CHOPPED FRESH BASIL

1 TABLESPOON FINELY CHOPPED FRESH PARSLEY

## DIRECTIONS

1. Place all of the ingredients, except for the basil and parsley, in a large saucepan and cook, stirring constantly, over medium heat until the tomatoes release their liquid and begin to break down, about 10 minutes. Reduce the heat to low and cook, stirring occasionally, for about 1½ hours, or until the flavor is to your liking.

2. Stir in the basil and parsley and season to taste. The sauce will be chunky. If you prefer a smoother texture, transfer the sauce to a blender and puree before serving.

# Pizza Dough

*Simple, versatile, and universally loved, pizza is the busy cook's best friend.*

## INGREDIENTS

2 CUPS WARM WATER (104 TO 112°F)

1 TABLESPOON ACTIVE DRY YEAST

2 TABLESPOONS SUGAR

1 TABLESPOON OLIVE OIL, PLUS MORE AS NEEDED

2½ CUPS "00" OR ALL-PURPOSE FLOUR, PLUS MORE FOR DUSTING

1 TEASPOON KOSHER SALT

## DIRECTIONS

1. Place the water, yeast, and sugar in a large mixing bowl and stir gently. Let the mixture sit until it begins to foam, about 7 to 10 minutes.

2. Add the olive oil to the mixture and stir. Add the flour and salt and work the mixture with your hands until the dough holds together. Remove the dough from the bowl and transfer it to a flour-dusted work surface. Knead the dough until it is smooth and springy, about 10 minutes. Grease a bowl with olive oil, place the dough in the bowl, cover with a kitchen towel, and store in a naturally warm spot until it has doubled in size, 1½ to 2 hours.

3. Place the dough on a flour-dusted work surface, cut it into two even pieces, and shape each piece into a smooth ball. If making pizza immediately, stretch the balls of dough into 10-inch rounds. If not using immediately, place in plastic bags and store in the refrigerator for up to 1 day and in the freezer for up to 2 weeks.

# CHAPTER 2

# IN A

# FLASH

---

*When most people picture a simple meal, the preparations in this chapter are what come to mind. Relying on minimal prep work and a skillet or saucepan placed over high heat, they are the ideal weeknight dinners, asking for very little of the little energy you have left and capable of providing satisfaction just minutes after you walk through the door.*

# Veal Scallopini

YIELD: **4 SERVINGS**

ACTIVE TIME: **10 MINUTES**

TOTAL TIME: **15 MINUTES**

*This is an unexpected Italian preparation. The veal will get slightly crispy, which is perfect alongside the meaty olives and the vibrant lemon juice. If you don't eat veal, try this with chicken.*

## INGREDIENTS

½ CUP ALL-PURPOSE FLOUR

½ TEASPOON GROUND NUTMEG

SALT AND PEPPER, TO TASTE

2 TABLESPOONS UNSALTED BUTTER

1 LB. VEAL CUTLETS, POUNDED THIN

½ CUP BEEF STOCK (SEE PAGE 15)

¼ CUP SLICED GREEN OLIVES

ZEST AND JUICE OF 1 LEMON

## DIRECTIONS

1. Warm a large cast-iron skillet over medium heat for 5 minutes.

2. Place the flour, nutmeg, salt, and pepper on a large plate and stir to combine.

3. Place the butter in the pan. When it starts to sizzle, dredge the veal in the seasoned flour until coated lightly on both sides. Working in batches, place the veal in the skillet and cook for about 1 minute on each side, until it is browned and the juices run clear. Set the cooked veal aside.

4. Deglaze the pan with the stock. Add the olives, lemon zest, and lemon juice, stir to combine, and cook until heated through.

5. To serve, plate the veal and pour some of the pan sauce over each cutlet.

# Pork Loin with Dried Cranberry Sauce

YIELD: **4 SERVINGS**

ACTIVE TIME: **20 MINUTES**

TOTAL TIME: **45 MINUTES**

*The beautiful, jewel-toned cranberries in this recipe are the ideal ornament for the rich flavor of the pork. Try serving this with baked sweet potatoes and roasted Brussels sprouts.*

## INGREDIENTS

2-LB PORK LOIN

2 TABLESPOONS COCONUT OIL

¾ CUP PORT WINE

2 TEASPOONS RED WINE VINEGAR

1 CUP DRIED CRANBERRIES

¼ CUP SUGAR

1 TEASPOON FINELY CHOPPED FRESH ROSEMARY (OPTIONAL)

½ TEASPOON BLACK PEPPER

3 TABLESPOONS UNSALTED BUTTER

## DIRECTIONS

1. Pat the pork loin dry and let it stand at room temperature for 10 minutes. Warm a large cast-iron skillet over medium heat. When it is warm, add the pork and cook until browned all over, about 10 minutes.

2. Reduce the heat to low and cook until the center of the pork loin registers 145°F on an instant-read thermometer, about 10 minutes. Remove the pork from the skillet and set it aside.

3. Add all of the remaining ingredients, except for the butter, to the skillet, stir to combine, and bring to a simmer. Cook until the cranberries are tender, about 5 minutes. Stir in the butter and remove the skillet from heat.

4. To serve, slice the pork loin and spoon the cranberry sauce over each slice.

# Garlic & Chili Broccolini

YIELD: **4 SERVINGS**

ACTIVE TIME: **15 MINUTES**

TOTAL TIME: **15 MINUTES**

*You can make this with broccoli, but the sweeter flavor of broccolini is a better match for the spice.*

## INGREDIENTS

½ LB. BROCCOLINI, TRIMMED

¼ CUP OLIVE OIL

2 GARLIC CLOVES, MINCED

SALT AND PEPPER, TO TASTE

1 TEASPOON RED PEPPER FLAKES

2 TABLESPOONS TOASTED ALMONDS, FOR GARNISH

## DIRECTIONS

1. Bring water to a boil in a cast-iron skillet or Dutch oven. Add the broccolini and cook for 30 seconds. Drain and transfer the broccolini to a paper towel–lined plate.

2. Warm the skillet or Dutch oven over medium-high heat and add the olive oil.

3. When the oil starts to smoke, add the broccolini and cook until well browned, about 5 minutes. Turn the broccolini over, add the garlic, season with salt and pepper, and toss to combine. When the broccolini is browned all over, add the red pepper flakes and toss to evenly distribute. Transfer to a serving platter, garnish with the toasted almonds, and serve immediately.

# Bacon & Zucchini Frittata

YIELD: **6 SERVINGS**

ACTIVE TIME: **10 MINUTES**

TOTAL TIME: **45 MINUTES**

*It turns out that crisp, salty bacon is the perfect complement to zucchini.*

## INGREDIENTS

¾ LB. THICK-CUT BACON, CHOPPED

1 SMALL ZUCCHINI, SLICED

1 GARLIC CLOVE, MINCED

4 OZ. GARLIC-HERB GOAT CHEESE

4 EGGS

½ LB. BABY SPINACH

1½ CUPS HALF-AND-HALF

½ TEASPOON KOSHER SALT

½ TEASPOON BLACK PEPPER

## DIRECTIONS

1. Preheat the oven to 350°F. Place the bacon in a 10-inch cast-iron skillet and cook over medium heat until crispy, about 8 minutes. Transfer the pieces to a paper towel–lined plate. Add the zucchini pieces and garlic to the skillet and cook until the zucchini is just soft, about 6 minutes. Return the pieces of bacon to the skillet, add the goat cheese, and stir until evenly distributed.

2. Whisk the eggs until scrambled. Add the spinach, half-and-half, salt, and pepper, and whisk to combine. Pour the egg mixture into the skillet and shake the skillet evenly to distribute.

3. Put the skillet in the oven and bake until the frittata is puffy and golden brown and the eggs are set, about 35 minutes. Remove from the oven and let the frittata sit for 10 minutes before slicing and serving.

# Peanut Butter & Bacon Oats

YIELD: **6 SERVINGS**

ACTIVE TIME: **5 MINUTES**

TOTAL TIME: **20 MINUTES**

*This combo may sound crazy at first, but the salty bacon, crunchy peanut butter, and creamy egg yolk work really well together.*

## INGREDIENTS

6 SLICES THICK-CUT BACON

6 EGGS

2 CUPS STEEL-CUT OATS

6 CUPS WATER

1 TABLESPOON KOSHER SALT

¼ CUP CRUNCHY PEANUT BUTTER

## DIRECTIONS

1. Place the bacon in a 12-inch cast-iron skillet and cook over medium heat until crispy, about 8 minutes. Transfer the bacon to a paper towel–lined plate, add the eggs to the skillet, and fry them in the bacon fat. Transfer the eggs to a plate and cover it loosely with aluminum foil to keep warm.

2. Wipe out the skillet, add the oats, water, and salt and cook over medium heat for 7 to 10 minutes, until the oats are tender.

3. While the oats are cooking, chop the bacon. Add the bacon and peanut butter to the oats and stir to incorporate. Ladle the oatmeal into warmed bowls, top each portion with a fried egg, and serve.

# Grandma Goodrich's Grits with Shrimp

YIELD: **8 SERVINGS**

ACTIVE TIME: **15 MINUTES**

TOTAL TIME: **1 HOUR**

*The beauty of cast-iron is on full display here, as it lends the bottom a gorgeous burnish.*

## INGREDIENTS

4 CUPS WATER

1 CUP QUICK-COOKING GRITS

2 LARGE EGGS

5 TABLESPOONS UNSALTED BUTTER, AT ROOM TEMPERATURE

¾ CUP MILK

SALT AND PEPPER, TO TASTE

1 LB. CHEDDAR CHEESE, GRATED

8 SLICES BACON

1 LB. SHRIMP, PEELED AND DEVEINED

4 SCALLIONS, TRIMMED AND SLICED

2 GARLIC CLOVES, MINCED

1 TABLESPOON FRESH LEMON JUICE

2 DASHES TABASCO (OPTIONAL)

## DIRECTIONS

1. Preheat the oven to 425°F. Place the water in a 12-inch cast-iron skillet or a Dutch oven and bring to a boil. While stirring constantly, slowly add the grits. Cover, reduce the heat to low, and cook, while stirring occasionally, until the grits are quite thick, about 5 minutes. Remove from heat.

2. Place the eggs, 4 tablespoons of the butter, and milk in a bowl, season with salt and pepper, and stir to combine. Stir the cooked grits into the egg mixture, add three-quarters of the cheese, and stir to incorporate.

3. Wipe out the pan, grease it with the remaining butter, and pour the mixture into the pan. Place in the oven and bake for 30 minutes. Remove, sprinkle the remaining cheese on top, and return the grits to the oven. Bake until the cheese is melted and the grits are firm, about 15 minutes. Remove from the oven and let cool for 10 minutes.

4. Place the bacon in a large skillet and cook over medium heat until crispy, about 8 minutes. Transfer the bacon to a paper towel–lined plate and place the shrimp in the skillet. Season with salt and pepper, cook for 1 minute, and turn the shrimp over. Cook for another minute, add the scallions, garlic, lime juice, and Tabasco (if using), toss to combine, and cook for another minute.

5. Divide the grits between four bowls, place a few shrimp on top of each portion, and then crumble the bacon over the shrimp.

# Crab & Okra Soup

YIELD: **4 SERVINGS**

ACTIVE TIME: **10 MINUTES**

TOTAL TIME: **30 MINUTES**

*If you're not already familiar, the combination of peanuts, coconut, and clam juice will be a revelation.*

## INGREDIENTS

1 CUP PEANUTS, CHOPPED

10 OKRA PODS, RINSED WELL
AND SLICED INTO ½-INCH ROUNDS

½ CUP COCONUT OIL

1 RED BELL PEPPER, STEMMED,
SEEDED, AND DICED

1 YELLOW ONION, SLICED INTO
HALF-MOONS

1 HABANERO PEPPER, STEMMED,
SEEDED, AND CHOPPED

1 LARGE POTATO, PEELED
AND DICED

4 CUPS VEGETABLE STOCK
(SEE PAGE 19)

1 CUP CLAM JUICE

1 CUP COCONUT MILK

SALT, TO TASTE

4 CUPS FRESH SPINACH LEAVES

1 LB. LUMP CRABMEAT

LIME WEDGES, FOR SERVING

## DIRECTIONS

1. Place the peanuts in a dry Dutch oven and toast over medium heat until they are browned, about 3 minutes. Remove them from the pot and set aside. Add the okra and cook, while stirring, until browned all over, about 5 minutes. Remove and set aside.

2. Place the coconut oil in the Dutch oven and warm over medium heat. When it starts to shimmer, add the bell pepper, onion, habanero pepper, and potato and sauté until the onion starts to soften, about 5 minutes.

3. Add the stock and clam juice, bring to a simmer, and cook for 5 minutes. Add the coconut milk, return to a simmer, and season with salt.

4. Working in batches, transfer the soup to a blender and puree until smooth. Return the soup to the Dutch oven and simmer for another 5 minutes. Stir in the peanuts, okra, spinach, and crabmeat and cook until the spinach has wilted, about 4 minutes. Ladle the soup into warmed bowls and serve with lime wedges.

# Succotash

YIELD: **4 SERVINGS**

ACTIVE TIME: **20 MINUTES**

TOTAL TIME: **50 MINUTES**

*Switching out the divisive lima bean for protein-rich edamame will make this a welcome sight on any table.*

## INGREDIENTS

8 SLICES BACON

1 CUP SLICED MUSHROOM CAPS

1 RED ONION, MINCED

4 CUPS CORN KERNELS

1 RED BELL PEPPER, STEMMED, SEEDED, AND DICED

2 CUPS FRESH OR FROZEN EDAMAME

1 TABLESPOON UNSALTED BUTTER

SALT AND PEPPER, TO TASTE

1 TABLESPOON FINELY CHOPPED FRESH MARJORAM

½ CUP FINELY CHOPPED FRESH BASIL

## DIRECTIONS

1. Place a large cast-iron skillet over medium heat, add the bacon, and cook until crispy, about 8 minutes. Transfer to a paper towel-lined plate to drain. Add the mushrooms to the skillet and cook until they release their liquid and start to brown, about 10 minutes. Reduce heat to low and cook until the mushrooms are a deep brown, about 15 minutes. While the mushrooms are cooking, chop the bacon into bite-sized pieces.

2. Add the onion, raise the heat to medium-high, and cook until it starts to soften, about 5 minutes. Add the corn, bell pepper, and edamame and cook, stirring often, until the corn is tender and bright yellow, about 4 minutes.

3. Add the butter and stir until it has melted and coated all of the vegetables. Season with salt and pepper, add the marjoram and basil, stir to incorporate, and serve.

# Spaghetti with Zucchini & Pesto

YIELD: **4 SERVINGS**

ACTIVE TIME: **10 MINUTES**

TOTAL TIME: **15 MINUTES**

*Slicing the zucchini extra thin makes it seem like there's twice as many noodles on the plate, and their freshness and crunch amplify everything else in the dish.*

## INGREDIENTS

SALT, TO TASTE

1 LB. SPAGHETTI OR FETTUCCINE

3 ZUCCHINI, SLICED VERY THIN WITH A MANDOLINE

2 TABLESPOONS UNSALTED BUTTER

BASIL PESTO (SEE PAGE 28)

## DIRECTIONS

1. Bring a large pot of salted water to a boil. When it is boiling, add the pasta and cook until it is nearly al dente, about 7 minutes. When the pasta has 1 minute left to cook, add the zucchini, and stir to combine.

2. Reserve ¼ cup of pasta water and then drain the pasta and zucchini. Return them to the pot, add the butter and the reserved pasta water, and cook over high heat until all of the water has been absorbed. Divide the pasta and zucchini between the plates and top each portion with the pesto.

# Omelet with Arugula, Ricotta, Sun-Dried Tomatoes & Olives

YIELD: **1 SERVING**

ACTIVE TIME: **5 MINUTES**

TOTAL TIME: **10 MINUTES**

*A perfect weeknight dinner for those nights when the other members of your household are out and about.*

## INGREDIENTS

3 EGGS

SALT, TO TASTE

1 TABLESPOON UNSALTED BUTTER

2 TABLESPOONS RICOTTA CHEESE

2 SUN-DRIED TOMATOES, SLICED

4 OIL-CURED OLIVES, PITTED AND ROUGHLY CHOPPED

1 HANDFUL ARUGULA

## DIRECTIONS

1. Crack the eggs into a bowl and whisk until scrambled. Season with salt.

2. Place the butter in a small nonstick skillet and melt over medium heat. When it starts to foam, add the eggs and swirl to coat the entire bottom of the pan. Let the eggs cook for 1 or 2 minutes, until the bottom starts to set.

3. Using a spatula, gently flip the omelet over and immediately place the ricotta, sun-dried tomatoes, and olives in the middle. Cook for 1 minute. Place a handful of arugula on top of the other ingredients and fold the omelet in half. Cook for another 30 seconds and serve.

# Veggie Burgers

YIELD : **4 SERVINGS**

ACTIVE TIME: **15 MINUTES**

TOTAL TIME: **45 MINUTES**

*Every chef worth their salt needs a foolproof veggie burger recipe such as this.*

## INGREDIENTS

1 (14 OZ.) CAN BLACK BEANS, DRAINED AND RINSED

⅓ CUP MINCED SCALLIONS

¼ CUP CHOPPED ROASTED RED PEPPERS

¼ CUP CORN KERNELS

1 CUP PANKO BREAD CRUMBS

1 EGG, LIGHTLY BEATEN

2 TABLESPOONS FINELY CHOPPED FRESH CILANTRO

½ TEASPOON CUMIN

½ TEASPOON CAYENNE PEPPER

½ TEASPOON BLACK PEPPER

1 TEASPOON FRESH LIME JUICE

1 TABLESPOON OLIVE OIL

HAMBURGER BUNS, FOR SERVING

GUACAMOLE (SEE PAGE 27) OR SLICED AVOCADO, FOR SERVING

## DIRECTIONS

1. Place half of the beans, the scallions, and roasted red peppers in a food processor and pulse until the mixture is a thick paste. Transfer to a large bowl.

2. Add the corn, bread crumbs, egg, cilantro, cumin, cayenne, black pepper, and lime juice to the bowl and stir to combine. Add the remaining beans and stir vigorously until the mixture holds together. Cover the bowl with plastic wrap and let it sit at room temperature for 30 minutes.

3. Place a 12-inch cast-iron skillet over medium-high heat and coat the bottom with the olive oil. Form the mixture into four patties. When the oil starts to shimmer, add the patties, cover the skillet, and cook until browned and cooked through, about 5 minutes per side. Serve immediately on hamburger buns with the Guacamole or sliced avocado.

# Dry-Fried Beans

YIELD: **4 SERVINGS**

ACTIVE TIME: **15 MINUTES**

TOTAL TIME: **25 MINUTES**

*If you can find Chinese pickled vegetables, use them, but know that kimchi will also work.*

## INGREDIENTS

1 TABLESPOON OLIVE OIL, PLUS MORE AS NEEDED

1 LB. GREEN BEANS, TRIMMED

½ LB. GROUND PORK

2 TABLESPOONS CHINESE PICKLED VEGETABLES OR KIMCHI (SEE PAGE 179 FOR HOMEMADE), CHOPPED

1 GARLIC CLOVE, CHOPPED

2 TABLESPOONS SHERRY

2 TABLESPOONS SOY SAUCE

1 TABLESPOON FERMENTED BLACK BEAN GARLIC SAUCE

1 TEASPOON SUGAR

WHITE RICE, FOR SERVING

## DIRECTIONS

1. Place the oil in a large skillet, warm over high heat, and add the beans. Let the beans sear on one side until they start to char, about 5 minutes. Stir and sear on the other side until they are well browned all over. Transfer to a bowl and set aside.

2. Add the pork to the pan and brown it over medium-high heat, while breaking it up with a wooden spoon, for about 6 minutes. Add the pickled vegetables or kimchi and the garlic. Cook, stirring continuously, until the contents of the pan are fragrant. Add more oil if the pan starts to look dry.

3. Add the Sherry and cook until it has nearly evaporated. Add the soy sauce, fermented black bean garlic sauce, and sugar and stir to incorporate.

4. Return the green beans to the pan, heat through, and serve with white rice.

# Lamb & Peas Curry

YIELD: **4 SERVINGS**

ACTIVE TIME: **15 MINUTES**

TOTAL TIME: **35 MINUTES**

*You can serve this dish with rice or put out some warm naan and scoop it up pita-style.*

## INGREDIENTS

1 TABLESPOON OLIVE OIL

1 ONION, CHOPPED

2 GARLIC CLOVES, MINCED

1-INCH PIECE FRESH GINGER, PEELED AND GRATED

1 LB. GROUND LAMB

1 TABLESPOON CURRY POWDER

½ CUP CHOPPED TOMATOES

1 CUP FROZEN PEAS

SALT, TO TASTE

2 TABLESPOONS PLAIN YOGURT

RICE, FOR SERVING (OPTIONAL)

NAAN, FOR SERVING (OPTIONAL)

## DIRECTIONS

1. Place the oil in a large skillet and warm over medium-high heat. When the starts to shimmer, add the onion and sauté until it starts to brown, about 10 minutes.

2. Add the garlic and ginger, cook for another 2 minutes, and then add the lamb, using a wooden spoon to break it up as it browns. Cook the lamb until fully browned, about 10 minutes.

3. Add the curry powder and stir to thoroughly incorporate. Cook for 1 minute, add the tomatoes, and cook until they start to collapse, about 5 minutes. Add the frozen peas and stir until they are warmed through. Season with salt, stir in the yogurt, and serve over rice or with naan.

# Tofu Tacos

YIELD: **4 SERVINGS**

ACTIVE TIME: **15 MINUTES**

TOTAL TIME: **20 MINUTES**

*The seasoning amounts should be used as a guide rather than a hard rule, depending on your spice threshold.*

## INGREDIENTS

1 TABLESPOON OLIVE OIL,
PLUS MORE AS NEEDED

1 LB. EXTRA-FIRM TOFU, DRAINED
AND CRUMBLED

1 TABLESPOON KOSHER SALT

1 TABLESPOON CUMIN

1 TABLESPOON GARLIC POWDER

1 TABLESPOON CAYENNE POWDER

ADOBO SAUCE, TO TASTE

CORN TORTILLAS, FOR SERVING

## DIRECTIONS

1. Place the oil in a large skillet and warm over medium-high heat. Once the oil is shimmering, add the tofu and all of the seasonings. Stir until the tofu is thoroughly coated and then cook until it starts to brown, about 10 minutes.

2. Add the adobo sauce and more oil if the pan looks dry. Cook for 5 more minutes and then serve with the corn tortillas and your favorite taco toppings.

# Green Shakshuka

YIELD: **4 SERVINGS**

ACTIVE TIME: **20 MINUTES**

TOTAL TIME: **30 MINUTES**

*Here, tomatillos add a tangy note to the mild spinach and eggs. The Tabasco is optional, but highly recommended to finish this dish off.*

## INGREDIENTS

1 TABLESPOON OLIVE OIL

1 ONION, CHOPPED

2 GARLIC CLOVES, MINCED

½ LB. TOMATILLOS, HUSKED, RINSED, AND CHOPPED

1 (12 OZ.) PACKAGE FROZEN CHOPPED SPINACH

1 TEASPOON CORIANDER

¼ CUP WATER

SALT AND PEPPER, TO TASTE

4 EGGS

TABASCO, FOR SERVING (OPTIONAL)

## DIRECTIONS

1. Place the oil in a large skillet and warm over medium-high heat. When the oil starts to shimmer, add the onion and sauté until just starting to soften, about 5 minutes. Add the garlic and cook until fragrant, about 2 minutes. Add the tomatillos and cook until they have collapsed, about 5 minutes.

2. Add the spinach, coriander, and water and cook, breaking up the spinach with a wooden spoon, until the spinach is completely thawed. Season with salt and pepper.

3. Evenly spread the mixture in the pan and then make four indentations in it. Crack an egg into each indentation. Reduce the heat to medium, cover the pan, and let the eggs cook until the whites are set, 3 to 5 minutes. Serve with Tabasco, if desired.

# Saag Aloo

YIELD: **4 SERVINGS**

ACTIVE TIME: **15 MINUTES**

TOTAL TIME: **30 MINUTES**

*A simple vegetable curry that never disappoints, and always impresses. In other words, a perfect dish for those nights when a friend drops by unexpectedly.*

## INGREDIENTS

1 TABLESPOON OLIVE OIL

½ LB. FINGERLING OR RED POTATOES, CHOPPED

1 SMALL ONION, CHOPPED

1 TEASPOON MUSTARD SEEDS

1 TEASPOON CUMIN

1 GARLIC CLOVE, CHOPPED

1-INCH PIECE FRESH GINGER, PEELED AND MINCED

1 LB. FROZEN CHOPPED SPINACH

1 TEASPOON RED PEPPER FLAKES

½ CUP WATER

SALT, TO TASTE

2 TABLESPOONS PLAIN YOGURT, OR TO TASTE

## DIRECTIONS

1. Place the oil and potatoes in a large skillet and cook over medium heat until the potatoes just start to brown, about 5 minutes.

2. Add the onion, mustard seeds, and cumin and cook until the onion starts to soften, about 5 minutes. Add the garlic and ginger and cook, stirring constantly, until fragrant, about 2 minutes.

3. Add the frozen spinach, the red pepper flakes, and water and cover the pan with a lid. Cook, stirring occasionally, until the spinach is heated through, about 10 minutes.

4. Remove the cover and cook until all of the liquid has evaporated. Season with salt, add the yogurt, and stir to incorporate. Add more yogurt if you prefer a creamier dish, stir to incorporate, and serve.

# BLT with Basil Mayo

YIELD: **2 SERVINGS**

ACTIVE TIME: **5 MINUTES**

TOTAL TIME: **5 MINUTES**

*It is the exquisite flavor of a summer-ripe tomato that makes this sandwich, but the basil mayonnaise is definitely in the running.*

## INGREDIENTS

**FOR THE BASIL MAYONNAISE**

½ CUP MAYONNAISE

½ CUP FRESH BASIL LEAVES

**FOR THE SANDWICHES**

4 SLICES BREAD

6 SLICES BACON, COOKED

4 LEAVES RED LEAF OR ROMAINE LETTUCE

2 RIPE TOMATOES, SLICED

SALT AND PEPPER, TO TASTE

## DIRECTIONS

1. To prepare the basil mayonnaise, place the mayonnaise and basil in a blender and puree until smooth. Set aside.

2. To begin preparations for the sandwiches, spread a layer of the basil mayonnaise on a slice of bread. Top with 3 slices of bacon, a leaf or two of lettuce, and as much tomato as desired. Season with salt and pepper.

3. Slather another piece of bread with the basil mayonnaise and place it on top of the slice of bread with the bacon and vegetables on it. Repeat to construct the second sandwich and serve.

# Coconut Curry Chicken with Basmati Rice

YIELD: **4 SERVINGS**

ACTIVE TIME: **20 MINUTES**

TOTAL TIME: **1 HOUR AND 15 MINUTES**

*The coconut milk tempers the spice just enough to ensure that your experience is pure pleasure.*

## INGREDIENTS

5 TABLESPOONS GREEN
CURRY PASTE

4 TO 6 BONELESS CHICKEN THIGHS

2 YELLOW ONIONS,
PEELED AND SLICED

2 RED BELL PEPPERS, STEMMED,
SEEDED, AND SLICED

3-INCH PIECE FRESH GINGER,
PEELED AND MASHED

1 GARLIC CLOVE, MASHED

3 TABLESPOONS FISH SAUCE

1 TABLESPOON MADRAS
CURRY POWDER

1 (14 OZ.) CAN COCONUT MILK

2 TABLESPOONS FINELY CHOPPED
THAI BASIL, PLUS MORE
FOR GARNISH

1½ CUPS BASMATI RICE

1 CUP WATER

LIME WEDGES, FOR SERVING

FRESH CILANTRO, FINELY
CHOPPED, FOR GARNISH

## DIRECTIONS

1.  Preheat the oven to 375°F. Rub 2 tablespoons of the green curry paste on the chicken and set aside for at least 30 minutes.

2.  Place a cast-iron skillet over medium-high heat and add the chicken thighs, skin-side down. Cook until the skin is crispy, turn over, and cook for another 3 minutes. Remove the chicken from the skillet and set aside.

3.  Add the onions, peppers, ginger, and garlic and cook, while stirring frequently and scraping the pan to remove any browned bits from the bottom, for 5 to 7 minutes.

4.  When the vegetables are tender, add the remaining green curry paste and cook for an additional 3 minutes, until fragrant.

5.  Add the fish sauce, curry powder, coconut milk, and Thai basil and stir until combined. Add the rice and water, stir to incorporate, and then return the chicken to the pan. Cover and transfer the pan to the oven. Bake until the rice is tender and has absorbed all of the liquid, about 25 minutes. Serve with the lime wedges and garnish with the cilantro and additional Thai basil.

## TARE SAUCE

Place ½ cup chicken stock (see page 12 for homemade), ½ cup soy sauce, ½ cup mirin, ¼ cup sake, ½ cup brown sugar, 2 smashed garlic cloves, 1 tablespoon minced ginger, and 2 sliced scallions in a small saucepan and bring to a simmer over low heat. Simmer for 10 minutes, stirring once or twice, and remove from heat. Let cool and strain before using.

# Chicken Tsukune

YIELD: **4 TO 6 SERVINGS**

ACTIVE TIME: **15 MINUTES**

TOTAL TIME: **30 MINUTES**

*Rich chicken thighs are essential here, as they ensure that the result is juicy and deeply flavorful.*

## INGREDIENTS

2 LBS. CHICKEN THIGHS, GROUND

1 LARGE EGG, LIGHTLY BEATEN

1 CUP PANKO BREAD CRUMBS

2 TEASPOONS WHITE MISO PASTE

2 TABLESPOONS SAKE

1½ TABLESPOONS MIRIN

½ TEASPOON BLACK PEPPER

TARE SAUCE (SEE SIDEBAR)

1½ SCALLIONS, TRIMMED AND SLICED, FOR GARNISH

SESAME SEEDS, FOR GARNISH

## DIRECTIONS

1. Place the ground chicken, egg, bread crumbs, miso, sake, mirin, and the pepper in a bowl and stir to combine. Cover the bowl and place it in the refrigerator while you make the sauce.

2. When the sauce has been prepared, remove the chicken mixture from the refrigerator and form it into compact pieces that are round or oblong.

3. Place a cast-iron grill pan over high heat and lightly coat with nonstick cooking spray.

4. When the pan is hot, add the meatballs and cook until they start to brown, about 3 minutes. Turn over and cook until they are completely cooked through, about 4 minutes. Remove from the pan and lightly baste the cooked meatballs with some of the Tare Sauce.

5. Garnish the meatballs with the scallions and sesame seeds and serve alongside the remaining Tare Sauce.

*Note: For a different presentation, thread the meatballs on skewers before adding them to the pan or placing them on a grill.*

# Sukiyaki

*This modest Japanese preparation will quickly become a family favorite.*

YIELD: **4 SERVINGS**

ACTIVE TIME: **5 MINUTES**

TOTAL TIME: **15 MINUTES**

## INGREDIENTS

SALT, TO TASTE

1½ LBS. UDON NOODLES

1 TABLESPOON OLIVE OIL

3 TABLESPOONS BROWN SUGAR

2 LBS. RIB EYE, SLICED VERY THIN

½ CUP MIRIN

½ CUP SAKE

⅓ CUP SOY SAUCE

1 CUP WATER

1 BUNCH SCALLIONS, TRIMMED AND SLICED INTO 2-INCH PIECES

2 CUPS CHOPPED NAPA CABBAGE

1 BUNCH ENOKI MUSHROOMS

6 LARGE SHIITAKE MUSHROOMS

1 CUP FRESH SPINACH

½ LB. TOFU, DRAINED AND DICED

## DIRECTIONS

1. Bring salted water to a boil in a Dutch oven. Add the noodles to the boiling water and cook for 2 minutes. Drain, rinse with cold water, and set the noodles aside.

2. Place the oil in the Dutch oven and warm over medium-high heat. When the oil starts to shimmer, add the brown sugar and steak and cook, while turning, until the steak is browned all over, about 2 minutes. Add the mirin, sake, soy sauce, and water and stir to combine.

3. Carefully submerge the noodles, scallions, cabbage, mushrooms, spinach, and tofu in the broth. Cover and steam until the cabbage is wilted, about 5 minutes. Ladle into warmed bowls and serve immediately.

*Tip: If you're having trouble getting the rib eye as thin as you'd like, place it in the freezer for 20 minutes before slicing it. This will make it much easier to cut into delicate slices.*

# Spicy Tonkatsu

YIELD: **4 SERVINGS**

ACTIVE TIME: **20 MINUTES**

TOTAL TIME: **25 MINUTES**

*This spicy take on a beloved Japanese dish is just as good cold for lunch the next day.*

## INGREDIENTS

1½ LBS. PORK CUTLETS

¼ CUP WASABI PASTE

¼ CUP OLIVE OIL

2 TABLESPOONS HORSERADISH

1 TABLESPOON FINELY CHOPPED FRESH PARSLEY

2 TABLESPOONS FINELY CHOPPED FRESH CHIVES

SALT AND PEPPER, TO TASTE

2 CUPS PANKO BREAD CRUMBS

LEMON WEDGES, FOR SERVING

## DIRECTIONS

1. Preheat the broiler on your oven. Pat the cutlets dry and lightly coat each one with the wasabi paste. In a bowl, combine 2 tablespoons of the olive oil, the horseradish, parsley, chives, salt, and pepper. Add the bread crumbs and carefully stir to coat. Set the seasoned panko aside.

2. Place a 12-inch cast-iron skillet over medium heat and coat the bottom with the remaining olive oil. When the oil starts to shimmer, add the pork cutlets and cook until golden brown, about 4 minutes. Flip the cutlets over and cook until golden brown on the other side, about 3 minutes.

3. Remove the cutlets from the skillet and dip each one into the seasoned panko until completely coated. Return the coated cutlets to the skillet. While keeping a close watch, place the pan under the broiler. Broil, turning the cutlets over once, until the crust is browned and crispy. Slice thin and serve with the lemon wedges.

# Bulgogi with Musaengchae

YIELD: **4 SERVINGS**

ACTIVE TIME: **5 MINUTES**

TOTAL TIME: **45 MINUTES**

*In Korean,* **bul** *means "fire" and* **gogi** *translates to "meat." When you come across a dish that trumpets such simplicity, you can be sure you've got a winner.*

## INGREDIENTS

2 LBS. PORK TENDERLOIN, SLICED THIN

4 GARLIC CLOVES, MINCED

1-INCH PIECE FRESH GINGER, PEELED AND MINCED

½ CUP GOCHUJANG (KOREAN CHILI PASTE)

2 TABLESPOONS SOY SAUCE

3 TABLESPOONS SESAME OIL

SESAME SEEDS, FOR GARNISH

2 SCALLIONS, TRIMMED AND CHOPPED, FOR GARNISH

MUSAENGCHAE (SEE SIDEBAR), FOR SERVING

## DIRECTIONS

1. Place all of the ingredients, except for the garnishes and Musaengchae, in a bowl and stir to combine. Let the meat marinate for at least 30 minutes and up to an hour.

2. Warm a 12-inch cast-iron skillet over high heat for 5 minutes. When it is extremely hot, add the marinated pork and sear, turning the pork as it browns, until it is cooked through, about 5 minutes.

3. Garnish with the sesame seeds and chopped green onions and serve with the Musaengchae.

---

### MUSAENGCHAE

Place 3 cups shredded daikon radish, 1 teaspoon gochugang powder, 2 tablespoons rice vinegar, 1 tablespoon kosher salt, and 1 tablespoon sugar in a mixing bowl and stir to combine. Let marinate for at least 1 hour before serving.

# Teriyaki Salmon with Vegetables

YIELD: **4 SERVINGS**

ACTIVE TIME: **20 MINUTES**

TOTAL TIME: **20 MINUTES**

*A great starting place if you've got a family full of folks who are wary of seafood.*

## INGREDIENTS

**FOR THE TERIYAKI SAUCE**

1-INCH PIECE FRESH GINGER, PEELED AND MINCED

3 GARLIC CLOVES, MINCED

1 TABLESPOON RICE VINEGAR

2 TABLESPOONS BROWN SUGAR

¼ CUP SOY SAUCE

1 TABLESPOON CORNSTARCH

½ CUP WATER

**FOR THE SALMON & VEGETABLES**

3 TABLESPOONS OLIVE OIL

4 CHINESE EGGPLANTS, SLICED INTO ½-INCH PIECES

1 RED BELL PEPPER, STEMMED, SEEDED, AND SLICED THIN

2 TABLESPOONS CHOPPED SCALLIONS

1 CUP BEAN SPROUTS

4 SALMON FILLETS

SALT AND PEPPER, TO TASTE

## DIRECTIONS

1. To prepare the teriyaki sauce, place all of the ingredients in a blender and puree until smooth. Transfer to a 12-inch cast-iron skillet and cook, while stirring, over medium heat until the sauce starts to thicken, about 6 minutes. Remove from heat and set aside.

2. Wipe out the skillet and preheat your oven to 375°F. To begin preparations for the salmon and vegetables, place the olive oil in the skillet and warm over medium-high heat. Add the eggplants, bell pepper, and scallions to the pan and cook, stirring occasionally, until the eggplants start to break down, about 5 minutes. Add the bean sprouts and stir to incorporate.

3. Place the salmon on top of the vegetables, skin-side down, season with salt, pepper, and some of the teriyaki sauce and transfer the pan to the oven. Bake until the salmon is cooked through, about 8 minutes, remove the pan from the oven, top with more of the teriyaki sauce, and serve.

# Red Snapper with Tomatillo Sauce

YIELD: **4 SERVINGS**

ACTIVE TIME: **10 MINUTES**

TOTAL TIME: **15 MINUTES**

*This recipe comes together in 15 minutes, but it's still as joyous and awe-inspiring as a fireworks show on the Fourth of July.*

## INGREDIENTS

1 LB. TOMATILLOS, HUSKED, RINSED, AND QUARTERED

½ WHITE ONION, CHOPPED

1 SERRANO PEPPER, STEMMED

1 GARLIC CLOVE, CRUSHED

1 BUNCH FRESH CILANTRO, SOME LEAVES RESERVED FOR GARNISH

2 TABLESPOONS OLIVE OIL

1½ LBS. SKINLESS RED SNAPPER FILLETS

RADISH, SLICED, FOR GARNISH

GUACAMOLE (SEE PAGE 27), FOR SERVING

CORN TORTILLAS, FOR SERVING

LIME WEDGES, FOR SERVING

## DIRECTIONS

1. Place a dry skillet over high heat and add the tomatillos, onion, and serrano pepper. Cook until the tomatillos and pepper are charred slightly, about 5 minutes, and then transfer the vegetables to a blender. Add the garlic and cilantro and puree until smooth.

2. Place the oil in a 12-inch cast-iron skillet and warm over medium-high heat. When the oil starts to shimmer, add the red snapper fillets in a single layer and cook until they brown lightly, about 3 to 4 minutes. Do not turn them over.

3. Remove the pan from heat and allow it to cool for a few minutes. Carefully pour the tomatillo sauce over the fish. It will immediately start to simmer. Place the skillet over medium-low heat and let it simmer until the fish is cooked through, about 4 minutes. Garnish with the reserved cilantro and sliced radish and serve with the Guacamole, tortillas, and lime wedges.

# Garlic Shrimp

YIELD: **4 SERVINGS**

ACTIVE TIME: **5 MINUTES**

TOTAL TIME: **10 MINUTES**

*What's not to like here? Sweet, briny shrimp, loads of luscious butter, and a bit of mellowed garlic, all held together by the acidic kick of lemon.*

## INGREDIENTS

4 TABLESPOONS UNSALTED BUTTER, AT ROOM TEMPERATURE

1 LB. SHRIMP, PEELED AND DEVEINED

8 GARLIC CLOVES, MINCED

½ TEASPOON LEMON-PEPPER SEASONING

1 TABLESPOON FRESH LEMON JUICE

1 TABLESPOON FINELY CHOPPED FRESH CHIVES OR PARSLEY, FOR GARNISH

## DIRECTIONS

1. Place a 10-inch cast-iron skillet over medium heat and add the butter.

2. When the butter has melted and is foaming, add the shrimp and cook, without stirring, for 3 minutes. Remove the shrimp from the pan with a slotted spoon and set them aside.

3. Reduce the heat to medium-low and add the garlic and lemon-pepper seasoning. Cook until the garlic has softened, about 3 minutes. Return the shrimp to the pan and cook until warmed through, about 1 minute. To serve, drizzle the lemon juice over the shrimp and garnish with the chives or parsley.

# Spring Pea Soup with Lemon Ricotta

YIELD: **4 SERVINGS**

ACTIVE TIME: **10 MINUTES**

TOTAL TIME: **20 MINUTES**

*Early in the spring, peas are absolutely perfect—tender enough that they don't require a long cook time and bursting with country-fresh flavor. Pair them with creamy, zesty lemon ricotta and you've got a dish that positively sings.*

## INGREDIENTS

1 CUP RICOTTA CHEESE

¼ CUP HEAVY CREAM

2 TABLESPOONS LEMON ZEST

1 TABLESPOON KOSHER SALT, PLUS 2 TEASPOONS

12 CUPS WATER

6 STRIPS LEMON PEEL

3 CUPS PEAS

3 SHALLOTS, DICED

6 FRESH MINT LEAVES, PLUS MORE FOR GARNISH

## DIRECTIONS

1. Place the ricotta, cream, lemon zest, and the 2 teaspoons of salt in a food processor and puree until smooth. Season to taste and set aside.

2. Place the water and remaining salt in a saucepan and bring to a boil over medium heat. Add the strips of lemon peel to the saucepan with the peas and shallots. Cook for 2 to 3 minutes, until the peas are just cooked through. Drain, making sure to reserve 2 cups of the cooking liquid, and immediately transfer the peas, strips of lemon peel, and shallots to a blender. Add the mint leaves and half of the reserved cooking liquid, and puree until the desired consistency is achieved, adding more cooking liquid as needed.

3. Season to taste, ladle into warmed bowls, and place a dollop of the lemon ricotta into each bowl. Garnish with additional mint and serve immediately, as the brilliant green color starts to fade as the soup cools.

# Mushroom Toast with Whipped Goat Cheese

YIELD: **4 SERVINGS**

ACTIVE TIME: **10 MINUTES**

TOTAL TIME: **35 MINUTES**

*Toast is as simple as it gets, but you'd be surprised by how well it cleans up.*

## INGREDIENTS

½ LB. MUSHROOMS (CHESTNUT RECOMMENDED), SLICED

2 TABLESPOONS OLIVE OIL

SALT, TO TASTE

4 THICK SLICES
SOURDOUGH BREAD

½ CUP HEAVY CREAM

4 OZ. GOAT CHEESE,
AT ROOM TEMPERATURE

½ CUP SUNFLOWER SEEDS

2 TABLESPOONS FRESH ROSEMARY

1 TABLESPOON HONEY

## DIRECTIONS

1.  Preheat the oven to 400°F. Place the mushrooms on a baking sheet, drizzle with half of the oil, and season with salt. Place the mushrooms in the oven and roast until they begin to darken, about 10 to 15 minutes. Place the slices of bread on another baking sheet, brush the tops with the remaining oil, and season with salt. Place the slices of bread in the oven and bake until golden brown, about 10 minutes.

2.  While the mushrooms and bread are in the oven, place the cream in a mixing bowl and beat until stiff peaks begin to form. Add the goat cheese and beat until well combined.

3.  Remove the mushrooms and bread from the oven and let cool for 5 minutes. Spread the cream-and-goat cheese mixture on the bread, top with the mushrooms, sunflower seeds, and rosemary, and drizzle the honey over the top.

# Thai Red Duck Curry

YIELD: **4 SERVINGS**

ACTIVE TIME: **15 MINUTES**

TOTAL TIME: **35 MINUTES**

*Your local grocery store will likely have precooked duck breasts available for purchase, but it's worth cooking your own just to have access to the rich, rendered fat that results from searing them.*

## INGREDIENTS

4 SKIN-ON DUCK BREASTS

¼ CUP THAI RED CURRY PASTE

2½ CUPS COCONUT MILK

10 MAKRUT LIME LEAVES (OPTIONAL)

1 CUP DICED PINEAPPLE

1 TABLESPOON FISH SAUCE, PLUS MORE TO TASTE

1 TABLESPOON BROWN SUGAR

6 BIRD'S EYE CHILI PEPPERS, STEMMED

20 CHERRY TOMATOES

1 CUP BASIL (THAI BASIL STRONGLY PREFERRED)

1½ CUPS COOKED JASMINE RICE, FOR SERVING

## DIRECTIONS

1. Use a very sharp knife to slash the skin on the duck breasts, while taking care not to cut all the way through to the meat.

2. Place a Dutch oven over medium-high heat. Place the duck breasts, skin-side down, in the pot and sear until browned, about 4 minutes. This will render a lot of the fat.

3. Turn the duck breasts over and cook until browned on the other side, about 4 minutes. Remove the duck from the pot, let cool, and drain the rendered duck fat. Reserve the duck fat for another preparation.

4. When the duck breasts are cool enough to handle, remove the skin and discard. Cut each breast into 2-inch pieces.

5. Set the heat to medium, add the curry paste to the Dutch oven, and sauté for 2 minutes. Add the coconut milk, bring to a boil, and cook for 5 minutes.

6. Reduce the heat, return the duck to the pot, and simmer for 8 minutes. Add the pineapple, fish sauce, brown sugar, and chilies, stir to incorporate, and simmer for 5 minutes. Skim any fat from the surface as the curry simmers. Taste and add more fish sauce if needed. Stir in the cherry tomatoes and basil and serve over the rice.

# CHAPTER 3

# LOW AND SLOW

*By utilizing long cook times and low temperatures, you can achieve startling results in the kitchen. These recipes take advantage of that tried-and-true formula, and frequently nothing more of you than collecting all of the ingredients in a cooking vessel, briefly stirring to combine, setting the temperature to low, and then proceeding with the various demands of the day as your mouthwatering meal slowly takes shape. Good food doesn't get any simpler, nor more satisfying, than that.*

# Sweet Potato Lentils

YIELD: **6 SERVINGS**

ACTIVE TIME: **10 MINUTES**

TOTAL TIME: **8 HOURS**

*Why should oatmeal get to hog the morning spotlight? Lentils are packed with fiber and protein, so you can get a complete meal in one shot.*

## INGREDIENTS

1 LB. BROWN LENTILS, RINSED

2 SWEET POTATOES, PEELED AND CHOPPED

¾ CUP HALF-AND-HALF

3¼ CUPS UNSWEETENED ALMOND MILK

4 CUPS UNSWEETENED CASHEW MILK

¼ CUP MAPLE SYRUP

1 TABLESPOON PURE VANILLA EXTRACT

1 TEASPOON ALLSPICE

ZEST OF 1 ORANGE

1 PINCH KOSHER SALT

CASHEWS, CRUSHED, FOR GARNISH

ALMONDS, CRUSHED, FOR GARNISH

## DIRECTIONS

1. Place all of the ingredients, except for the garnishes, in a slow cooker and stir to combine.

2. Cook on low until the lentils and sweet potatoes have broken down and the mixture is smooth, about 8 hours. Ladle into bowls and garnish with the crushed almonds and cashews.

# Dal

*This simple stew of yellow peas, orange lentils, or mung beans is an everyday staple in most of India.*

## INGREDIENTS

2 TABLESPOONS OLIVE OIL

1 YELLOW ONION, CHOPPED

2 GARLIC CLOVES, MINCED

2 TEASPOONS RED PEPPER FLAKES

2 CURRY LEAVES (OPTIONAL)

1 TEASPOON KOSHER SALT

1½ CUPS YELLOW SPLIT PEAS, SORTED AND RINSED

4 CUPS WATER

1 TEASPOON TURMERIC

1 CUP PEAS

## DIRECTIONS

1. Place the olive oil in a Dutch oven and warm over medium-high heat. Add the onion, garlic, red pepper flakes, curry leaves (if using), and salt and sauté until the onion is translucent, about 3 minutes.

2. Add the yellow split peas, water, and turmeric and bring to a simmer. Cover and gently simmer for 1 hour, stirring the dal two or three times as it cooks.

3. Remove the lid and simmer, while stirring occasionally, until the dal has thickened, about 30 minutes. When the dal has the consistency of porridge, stir in the peas, and cook until they are warmed through. Ladle the dal into warmed bowls and serve.

## INGREDIENTS

1½ LBS. CHUCK STEAK,
CUT INTO 1-INCH PIECES

2 TABLESPOONS KOSHER SALT

1 TABLESPOON BLACK PEPPER

1 TABLESPOON GRANULATED
ONION

1 TABLESPOON GRANULATED
GARLIC

½ TABLESPOON DRIED OREGANO

1 TEASPOON CELERY SEEDS

1 PINCH RED PEPPER FLAKES

2 TABLESPOONS FINELY CHOPPED
FRESH THYME

2 BAY LEAVES

4 CUPS BEEF STOCK (SEE PAGE 15)

3 GARLIC CLOVES, MINCED

3 CARROTS, PEELED AND CHOPPED

2 LEEKS, TRIMMED, RINSED WELL,
AND CHOPPED

1 YELLOW ONION, CHOPPED

2 YUKON GOLD POTATOES, PEELED
AND CHOPPED

2 CELERY STALKS, CHOPPED

3 OZ. TOMATO PASTE

2 TABLESPOONS
WORCESTERSHIRE SAUCE

1 TABLESPOON SOY SAUCE

¼ CUP ALL-PURPOSE FLOUR

# Beef Stew

*This perfectly captures the beauty of the slow cooker: prepare it the night before, set on low before leaving in the morning, and come home to a house that smells amazing and a meal that's ready to go.*

## DIRECTIONS

1. Place all of the ingredients, except for 1 cup of the stock and the flour, in a slow cooker and stir to combine.

2. Place the flour and remaining stock in a bowl and stir until smooth. Add this mixture to the slow cooker and cover. Cook on low until the beef and potatoes are tender, 6 to 8 hours.

# Moroccan Lentil Stew

YIELD: **6 SERVINGS**

ACTIVE TIME: **10 MINUTES**

TOTAL TIME: **8 HOURS**

*The vegetable stock and lemon juice provide a lightness that gives this dish a wonderful lift.*

## INGREDIENTS

1 CUP BROWN LENTILS

½ CUP FRENCH LENTILS

4 CUPS VEGETABLE STOCK
(SEE PAGE 19)

3 CARROTS, RINSED WELL
AND CHOPPED

1 LARGE WHITE ONION, CHOPPED

3 GARLIC CLOVES, MINCED

3-INCH PIECE FRESH GINGER,
PEELED AND MINCED

ZEST AND JUICE OF 1 LEMON

3 TABLESPOONS SMOKED PAPRIKA

2 TABLESPOONS CINNAMON

1 TABLESPOON GROUND
CORIANDER

1 TABLESPOON TURMERIC

1 TABLESPOON CUMIN

1½ TEASPOONS ALLSPICE

2 TO 3 BAY LEAVES

SALT AND PEPPER, TO TASTE

1 (14 OZ.) CAN CANNELLINI BEANS

FRESH MINT, FINELY CHOPPED,
FOR GARNISH

GOAT CHEESE, CRUMBLED,
FOR GARNISH

## DIRECTIONS

1. Place the lentils in a fine sieve and rinse to remove any impurities. Place all of the ingredients, save the cannellini beans and the garnishes, in a slow cooker. Cover and cook on low for 7½ hours.

2. After 7½ hours, add the cannellini beans. Stir, cover, and cook for 30 minutes. Garnish with fresh mint and goat cheese and serve.

# Hungarian Goulash

YIELD: **6 TO 8 SERVINGS**

ACTIVE TIME: **30 MINUTES**

TOTAL TIME: **2 HOURS AND 30 MINUTES**

*A rich and hearty dish that will be even better the next day. Redolent with the flavors of Eastern Europe—sweet paprika, earthy caraway, garlic, and sour cream—it is the comfort food you never knew you needed.*

## INGREDIENTS

2 TABLESPOONS OLIVE OIL

3 LBS. CHUCK STEAK, TRIMMED

3 YELLOW ONIONS, CHOPPED

2 CARROTS, PEELED AND CHOPPED

2 BELL PEPPERS, STEMMED, SEEDED, AND CHOPPED

1 TEASPOON CARAWAY SEEDS

¼ CUP ALL-PURPOSE FLOUR

3 TABLESPOONS SWEET HUNGARIAN PAPRIKA

3 TABLESPOONS TOMATO PASTE

2 GARLIC CLOVES, MINCED

1 TEASPOON SUGAR

SALT AND PEPPER, TO TASTE

2 CUPS BEEF STOCK (SEE PAGE 15)

1 LB. WIDE EGG NOODLES

1 CUP SOUR CREAM

## DIRECTIONS

1. Place the oil in a Dutch oven and warm over medium heat. When the oil starts to smoke, add the meat in batches and cook until it is browned all over, taking care not to crowd the pot. Remove the browned meat and set aside.

2. Reduce the heat to medium-low. Wait 2 minutes and then add the onions, carrots, and peppers. Stir to coat with the pan drippings and sauté the vegetables until they are golden brown, about 10 minutes. Add the caraway seeds, stir to incorporate, and cook until the seeds are fragrant, about 1 minute.

3. Add the flour, paprika, tomato paste, garlic, sugar, salt, and pepper and stir to incorporate. Add the stock and use a wooden spoon to scrape up any browned bits from the bottom of the pan.

4. Bring the goulash to a boil, then reduce the heat and let it simmer until it thickens slightly, about 10 minutes. Return the meat to the Dutch oven, cover, and simmer over low heat until the meat is very tender, about 2 hours.

5. Approximately 20 minutes before the goulash will be done, bring water to a boil in a large pot. Add the egg noodles to the boiling water and cook until al dente. Drain and set aside.

6. To serve, stir in the sour cream and ladle the goulash over the cooked egg noodles.

# Ratatouille

---

YIELD: **4 SERVINGS**

ACTIVE TIME: **20 MINUTES**

TOTAL TIME: **2 HOURS**

*Some people think sausage is an essential ingredient in a traditional ratatouille, but when your garden is at its peak, this dish has enough flavor to carry on without it.*

## INGREDIENTS

⅓ CUP OLIVE OIL

6 GARLIC CLOVES, MINCED

1 EGGPLANT, CHOPPED

2 ZUCCHINI, SLICED INTO HALF-MOONS

2 BELL PEPPERS, STEMMED, SEEDED, AND CHOPPED

4 TOMATOES, SEEDED AND CHOPPED

SALT AND PEPPER, TO TASTE

## DIRECTIONS

1. Place a 12-inch cast-iron skillet over medium-high heat and add half of the olive oil. When the oil starts to shimmer, add the garlic and eggplant and cook, while stirring, until pieces are coated with oil and just starting to sizzle, about 2 minutes.

2. Reduce the heat to medium, add the zucchini, peppers, and remaining oil, and stir to combine. Cover the skillet and cook, while stirring occasionally, until the eggplant, zucchini, and peppers are almost tender, about 15 minutes.

3. Add the tomatoes, stir to combine, and cook until the eggplant, zucchini, and peppers are tender and the tomatoes have collapsed, about 25 minutes. Remove the skillet from heat, season with salt and pepper, and allow to sit for at least 1 hour. Reheat before serving.

# Halibut with Braised Vegetables

YIELD: **4 SERVINGS**

ACTIVE TIME: **30 MINUTES**

TOTAL TIME: **1 HOUR**

*The kale is key to this one, as it provides a nice soft bed for the halibut and ensures that it remains moist and full of flavor.*

## INGREDIENTS

¼ CUP OLIVE OIL

1 YELLOW BELL PEPPER, STEMMED, SEEDED, AND CHOPPED

1 RED BELL PEPPER, STEMMED, SEEDED, AND CHOPPED

1 HABANERO PEPPER, PIERCED

2 SMALL WHITE SWEET POTATOES

1 CUP CHOPPED RED CABBAGE

SALT AND PEPPER, TO TASTE

3 GRAFFITI EGGPLANTS, CUT INTO 2-INCH PIECES

2-INCH PIECE FRESH GINGER, PEELED AND MASHED

4 GARLIC CLOVES, MINCED

2 TABLESPOONS GREEN CURRY PASTE

3 BABY BOK CHOY, CHOPPED

4 CUPS FISH STOCK (SEE PAGE 16)

2 TABLESPOONS SWEET PAPRIKA

2 TABLESPOONS FINELY CHOPPED FRESH CILANTRO

3 (14 OZ.) CANS COCONUT MILK

2 BUNCHES TUSCAN KALE, STEMS REMOVED, LEAVES TORN

1½ LBS. HALIBUT FILLETS

SCALLIONS, CHOPPED, FOR GARNISH

## DIRECTIONS

1. Place the olive oil in a Dutch oven and warm over medium-high heat. When the oil starts to shimmer, add the bell peppers, habanero pepper, sweet potatoes, and cabbage. Season with salt and pepper and cook, while stirring, until the sweet potatoes begin to caramelize, about 6 minutes.

2. Add the eggplants, ginger, and garlic and cook, stirring frequently, until the eggplants begin to collapse, about 10 minutes. Add the curry paste and stir to coat all of the vegetables. Cook until the mixture is fragrant, about 2 minutes.

3. Add the bok choy, stock, paprika, cilantro, and coconut milk and cook until the liquid has reduced by one-quarter, about 20 minutes.

4. Add the kale to the Dutch oven. Place the halibut fillets on top of the kale, reduce the heat to medium, cover, and cook until the fish is cooked through, about 10 minutes.

5. Remove the Dutch oven's cover, remove the habanero, and discard it. Ladle the vegetables and the sauce into the bowls and top each portion with a halibut fillet. Garnish with the scallions and serve.

# Bigos

YIELD: **4 SERVINGS**

ACTIVE TIME: **20 MINUTES**

TOTAL TIME: **1 HOUR AND 30 MINUTES**

*The combination of cabbage, onion, and noodles may sound plain, but the deeply browned vegetables have a subtle smoky sweetness, while the sturdy egg noodles provide a satisfying chewiness. It is pure comfort food.*

## INGREDIENTS

2 TABLESPOONS OLIVE OIL

½ LB. KIELBASA, DICED

6½ TABLESPOONS UNSALTED BUTTER

2 LARGE ONIONS, DICED

SALT AND PEPPER, TO TASTE

1½ LBS. GREEN CABBAGE, CORED AND DICED

¾ LB. WIDE EGG NOODLES

## DIRECTIONS

1. Warm a large skillet over medium heat for 1 minute. Add the oil and raise heat to medium-high. When the oil starts shimmering, add the kielbasa and cook, stirring occasionally, until it starts to brown, 3 to 5 minutes. Use a slotted spoon to transfer the kielbasa to a small bowl.

2. Add 3 tablespoons of the butter to the skillet. When it has melted and stopped foaming, add the onions and a couple pinches of salt and cook, stirring frequently, until softened, 8 to 10 minutes. Add another 3 tablespoons of the butter, the cabbage, a few more pinches of salt, and a few pinches of pepper and stir to combine. When the mixture starts sizzling, cover and reduce the heat to low. Cook, stirring occasionally, until the cabbage is very soft and a deep golden brown, 45 minutes to 1 hour.

3. As the onions and cabbage cook, bring a large pot of water to a boil. When it's boiling, add salt (1 tablespoon for every 4 cups water) and stir. Add the egg noodles and stir for the first minute to prevent any sticking. Cook them according to the package instructions. Reserve ¼ cup of the pasta water and drain the noodles.

4. Return the pot to the stove. Immediately turn the heat to high and add the remaining butter and the reserved pasta water. Add the drained noodles and toss to combine. Once the added water has been absorbed by the noodles, add the kielbasa and onion-and-cabbage mixture and toss to evenly distribute. Cook for 1 to 2 minutes, gently stirring so as to not tear the noodles. Season to taste and serve immediately.

# Spinach & Mushroom Quinoa

YIELD: **6 SERVINGS**

ACTIVE TIME: **20 MINUTES**

TOTAL TIME: **5 HOURS**

*Folding in the herbs at the end of your preparation packs this dish with tons of fresh flavor.*

## INGREDIENTS

1½ CUPS QUINOA, RINSED

2½ CUPS VEGETABLE STOCK
(SEE PAGE 19)

1 YELLOW ONION, CHOPPED

½ RED BELL PEPPER, STEMMED,
SEEDED, AND CHOPPED

¾ LB. PORTOBELLO MUSHROOMS,
CHOPPED

2 GARLIC CLOVES, MINCED

1 TABLESPOON KOSHER SALT,
PLUS MORE TO TASTE

1 TABLESPOON BLACK PEPPER,
PLUS MORE TO TASTE

3 CUPS BABY SPINACH

1½ CUPS FRESH BASIL LEAVES,
FINELY CHOPPED

¼ CUP FINELY CHOPPED
FRESH DILL

2 TABLESPOONS FINELY CHOPPED
FRESH THYME

## DIRECTIONS

1. Place all of the ingredients, except for the spinach and fresh herbs, in a slow cooker and cook on high until the quinoa is slightly fluffy, about 4 hours.

2. Add the spinach and turn off the heat. Keep the slow cooker covered and let sit for 1 hour.

3. Fluff the quinoa with a fork, add the basil, dill, and thyme, and fold to incorporate. Season with salt and pepper and serve.

# Chicken & Sausage Cacciatore

YIELD: **6 SERVINGS**

ACTIVE TIME: **15 MINUTES**

TOTAL TIME: **6 HOURS AND 30 MINUTES**

## INGREDIENTS

1 LB. SWEET ITALIAN SAUSAGE

2 LBS. BONELESS, SKINLESS CHICKEN THIGHS

1 (28 OZ.) CAN WHOLE SAN MARZANO TOMATOES

1 (28 OZ.) CAN DICED TOMATOES

⅔ CUP DRY RED WINE

4 SHALLOTS, CHOPPED

3 GARLIC CLOVES, MINCED

1 GREEN BELL PEPPER, STEMMED, SEEDED, AND CHOPPED

1 RED, YELLOW, OR ORANGE BELL PEPPER, STEMMED, SEEDED, AND CHOPPED

1 TABLESPOON DRIED OREGANO

1 TABLESPOON GRANULATED GARLIC

1 TABLESPOON SUGAR

2 TABLESPOONS KOSHER SALT, PLUS MORE TO TASTE

½ TEASPOON RED PEPPER FLAKES

1 CUP WHITE RICE

BLACK PEPPER, TO TASTE

1 TABLESPOON FINELY CHOPPED FRESH OREGANO, FOR GARNISH

PARMESAN CHEESE, GRATED, FOR GARNISH

*Tender chicken thighs, Italian sausage soft enough to cut with a fork, oregano, and a scoop of salty Parmesan cheese combine to create a mouthwatering main course.*

## DIRECTIONS

1. Place all of the ingredients, except for the white rice, black pepper, and the garnishes, in a slow cooker. Cook on low for 5½ hours.

2. Add the rice to the slow cooker, raise heat to high, and cook until the rice is tender, 40 to 50 minutes. The cooking time may vary depending on your slow cooker, so be sure to check on the rice after about 30 minutes to avoid overcooking.

3. Season with salt and pepper, garnish with the oregano and a generous amount of Parmesan, and serve.

# Shredded Chicken with Beans & Rice

YIELD: **6 SERVINGS**

ACTIVE TIME: **10 MINUTES**

TOTAL TIME: **5 HOURS**

*The cumin provides earthiness, the jalapeño provides a bit of heat, and they combine to add depth to what should be a simple bowl of chicken and rice.*

## INGREDIENTS

2 LBS. BONELESS, SKINLESS CHICKEN BREASTS

1 CUP CHICKEN STOCK (SEE PAGE 12)

1 JALAPEÑO PEPPER, STEMMED, SEEDED, AND MINCED, PLUS MORE FOR GARNISH

2 GARLIC CLOVES, MINCED

1½ TABLESPOONS CUMIN

1 TABLESPOON GRANULATED GARLIC

1 CUP WHITE RICE

2 PLUM TOMATOES, CHOPPED

2 TABLESPOONS KOSHER SALT

1 TABLESPOON BLACK PEPPER

1 (14 OZ.) CAN BLACK BEANS, DRAINED

## DIRECTIONS

1. Place the chicken, stock, jalapeño, garlic, cumin, and granulated garlic in a slow cooker and cook on high until the chicken is very tender and falling apart, about 4 hours. Remove the chicken from the slow cooker, place it in a bowl, and shred it with a fork. Cover the bowl with aluminum foil and set it aside.

2. Add the rice, tomatoes, salt, and black pepper to the slow cooker and cook until the rice is tender, 40 to 50 minutes. Make sure to check on the rice after 30 minutes, since cook times will vary between different brands of slow cookers.

3. Add the black beans to the slow cooker, stir to combine, top with the shredded chicken, and cover until warmed through. Garnish with additional jalapeño and serve.

# Chili con Carne

YIELD: **6 SERVINGS**

ACTIVE TIME: **10 MINUTES**

TOTAL TIME: **24 HOURS**

*Save this for a Sunday during football season: it's so good, it won't even matter if your team ends up losing.*

## INGREDIENTS

1½ LBS. GROUND BEEF

1 (28 OZ.) CAN CRUSHED SAN MARZANO TOMATOES

1 RED BELL PEPPER, STEMMED, SEEDED, AND CHOPPED

2 SMALL YELLOW ONIONS, CHOPPED, PLUS MORE FOR GARNISH

4 GARLIC CLOVES, MINCED

1 JALAPEÑO PEPPER, STEMMED, SEEDED, AND MINCED

1 LB. PINTO BEANS, SOAKED OVERNIGHT AND DRAINED

¼ CUP CHOPPED FRESH CILANTRO, PLUS MORE FOR GARNISH

¼ CUP HOT SAUCE

2 TABLESPOONS CHILI POWDER

1 TABLESPOON BLACK PEPPER

1 TABLESPOON KOSHER SALT

2 TABLESPOONS GRANULATED GARLIC

⅓ CUP CUMIN

1 TABLESPOON MADRAS CURRY POWDER

1 TABLESPOON DRIED OREGANO

CHEDDAR CHEESE, GRATED, FOR GARNISH

## DIRECTIONS

1. Place the ground beef in a Dutch oven and cook, while breaking it up with a wooden spoon, over medium heat until it is browned, about 10 minutes.

2. Drain off the fat, add all of the remaining ingredients, except for the garnishes, and stir to combine. Bring to a boil, reduce heat so that the chili gently simmers, and cook until the beans are fork-tender and the flavor is to your liking, 3 to 4 hours. Ladle into warmed bowls and garnish with the cheddar cheese and the additional onion and cilantro.

## DRY RUB

Place ¼ cup ground coffee, 1 teaspoon coriander, 2 teaspoons black pepper, a pinch of red pepper flakes, 1 teaspoon cumin, 2 teaspoons mustard powder, 2 teaspoons dark chili powder, 1 teaspoon paprika, 6 tablespoons kosher salt, and 6 tablespoons light brown sugar in a mixing bowl and stir to combine. Store in an airtight container for up to 6 months.

# Coffee & Bourbon Brisket

YIELD: **6 SERVINGS**

ACTIVE TIME: **15 MINUTES**

TOTAL TIME: **8 HOURS AND 30 MINUTES**

## INGREDIENTS

**FOR THE BRISKET**

1 YELLOW ONION, CHOPPED

1 PEACH, PEELED AND CHOPPED

1 NECTARINE, PEELED AND CHOPPED

2-INCH PIECE FRESH GINGER, PEELED AND MINCED

½ CUP DRY RUB (SEE SIDEBAR)

3½ LBS. FLAT-CUT BRISKET

1 CUP WATER

**FOR THE BBQ SAUCE**

2 CUPS BREWED COFFEE

¼ CUP DARK BROWN SUGAR

¾ CUP BOURBON

3 TABLESPOONS MOLASSES

¼ CUP APPLE CIDER VINEGAR

2 TABLESPOONS WORCESTERSHIRE SAUCE

¼ CUP KETCHUP

1 TABLESPOON GRANULATED GARLIC

½ TABLESPOON BLACK PEPPER

1 TABLESPOON TAPIOCA STARCH OR CORNSTARCH

*You'll learn to love this marriage of Texan and Southern BBQ, where the slight bitterness of coffee and sweet bourbon work beautifully together.*

## DIRECTIONS

1. To prepare the brisket, place the onion, peach, nectarine, and ginger in a slow cooker. Apply the Dry Rub to the brisket and place the brisket on top of the mixture in the slow cooker. Add the water, cover, and cook on low for 6 hours.

2. Remove the contents of the slow cooker, transfer the brisket to a cutting board, and discard everything else. To prepare the BBQ sauce, place all of the ingredients in the slow cooker and cook on high for 1 hour.

3. Return the brisket to the slow cooker, reduce the heat to low, and cook for another hour. Remove the brisket from the slow cooker, let rest for 30 minutes, and then use a sharp knife to cut it into ½-inch-thick slices, making sure to cut against the grain.

# Chipotle Sausage & Peppers

YIELD: **6 SERVINGS**

ACTIVE TIME: **10 MINUTES**

TOTAL TIME: **4 HOURS**

*The smoky bite of the chipotle peppers puts a new twist on a ballpark favorite.*

## INGREDIENTS

5 BELL PEPPERS, STEMMED, SEEDED, AND SLICED

1 (28 OZ.) CAN FIRE-ROASTED TOMATOES

3 GARLIC CLOVES

2 CHIPOTLE PEPPERS IN ADOBO

1 TABLESPOON ADOBO SAUCE

2 LBS. KIELBASA, CUT INTO 6 PIECES

1 HABANERO PEPPER, PIERCED

SUBMARINE ROLLS, FOR SERVING (OPTIONAL)

## DIRECTIONS

1. Place the bell peppers in a slow cooker and set it to high heat. Place the tomatoes, garlic, chipotles in adobo, and adobo sauce in a blender and puree until smooth. Pour the puree over the peppers and stir to combine.

2. Add the kielbasa and the habanero to the slow cooker, cover, and cook on high for 4 hours.

3. Discard the habanero. Ladle the contents of the slow cooker into warmed bowls or submarine rolls and serve immediately.

# Braised Lamb with Minty Peas

YIELD: **4 TO 6 SERVINGS**

ACTIVE TIME: **30 MINUTES**

TOTAL TIME: **4 HOURS**

*Don't hesitate to splurge on the best lamb you can find—this dish is so simple that extra cost is certain to shine through.*

## INGREDIENTS

2 TABLESPOONS OLIVE OIL

5-LB., BONE-IN LAMB SHOULDER

SALT, TO TASTE

1 SMALL ONION, CHOPPED

2 CARROTS, PEELED AND CHOPPED

3 BAY LEAVES

2 TABLESPOONS BLACK PEPPERCORNS

2 CUPS WATER

2 SPRIGS FRESH ROSEMARY

3 SPRIGS FRESH MINT

3 CUPS PEAS

## DIRECTIONS

1. Preheat the oven to 300°F. Place the oil in a Dutch oven and warm it over medium-high heat. Season all sides of the lamb shoulder liberally with salt. When the oil starts to glisten, place the lamb in the pan and cook, turning occasionally, until it is browned on all sides.

2. Place the onion, carrots, bay leaves, peppercorns, water, and rosemary in the Dutch oven. Cover, place in the oven, and braise until the lamb is fork-tender, about 3½ hours.

3. When the lamb shoulder is close to ready, place the sprigs of mint and peas in a saucepan and cover with water. Cook over medium heat until the peas are tender, approximately 4 minutes for fresh peas and 7 minutes if using frozen. Drain, discard the mint, and serve the peas alongside the lamb shoulder.

# Rogan Josh

YIELD: **4 SERVINGS**

ACTIVE TIME: **20 MINUTES**

TOTAL TIME: **1 HOUR AND 30 MINUTES**

*Pressed for time? This can also be a fantastic make-ahead dish that tastes just as good—if not better—the next day.*

## INGREDIENTS

¼ CUP OLIVE OIL

2 LBS. BONELESS LAMB SHOULDER, CUT INTO 1-INCH PIECES

SALT, TO TASTE

2 LARGE YELLOW ONIONS, SLICED THIN

2-INCH PIECE FRESH GINGER, PEELED AND MINCED

2 GARLIC CLOVES, MINCED

1 TABLESPOON CURRY POWDER, PLUS 1 TEASPOON

1 TEASPOON TURMERIC

1 TEASPOON CAYENNE PEPPER, OR TO TASTE

1 TEASPOON GARAM MASALA

1 (14 OZ.) CAN CRUSHED TOMATOES

1 CUP PLAIN YOGURT

2 CUPS WATER

FRESH CILANTRO, FINELY CHOPPED, FOR GARNISH

RED ONION, MINCED, FOR GARNISH

## DIRECTIONS

1. Place the oil in a Dutch oven and warm over high heat. Generously season the lamb with salt. When the oil starts to shimmer, add the lamb and cook, turning occasionally, until it is lightly browned all over, about 12 minutes. Remove with a slotted spoon and set aside.

2. Add the yellow onions, ginger, garlic, curry powder, turmeric, cayenne, and garam masala to the Dutch oven and sauté for 2 minutes. Add the tomatoes, yogurt, and water and bring to a gentle boil. Return the lamb to the pot, reduce the heat, cover, and simmer until the lamb is very tender, about 1 hour. Remove the cover occasionally to stir and make sure the rogan josh does not burn.

3. Ladle into warmed bowls and garnish with the cilantro and red onion.

# Yankee Short Ribs

YIELD: **4 SERVINGS**

ACTIVE TIME: **30 MINUTES**

TOTAL TIME: **4 HOURS AND 30 MINUTES**

*Revive a New England classic—the Yankee Pot Roast—by utilizing the short rib, a underutilized and sublime cut of beef.*

## INGREDIENTS

2 TABLESPOONS OLIVE OIL

4 LBS. SHORT RIBS

SALT AND PEPPER, TO TASTE

2 LARGE ONIONS, SLICED

4 CARROTS, CHOPPED

4 LARGE POTATOES, CHOPPED

8 CUPS BEEF STOCK (SEE PAGE 15)

4 BAY LEAVES

2 SPRIGS FRESH ROSEMARY

2 SPRIGS FRESH THYME

½ CUP RED WINE

## DIRECTIONS

1. Preheat the oven to 300°F. Place the oil in a large skillet and warm it over medium-high heat. Pat the short ribs dry and season generously with salt. Working in batches, place the short ribs in the skillet and cook, while turning, until they are browned all over.

2. Place the browned short ribs in a Dutch oven along with the onions, carrots, potatoes, stock, and bay leaves. Cover, place in the oven, and cook until the short ribs are fork-tender and the meat easily comes away from the bone, about 4 hours. Remove from the oven, strain through a fine sieve, and reserve the cooking liquid.

3. Place the reserved liquid in a pan with the rosemary, thyme, and red wine. Cook over high heat until the mixture has reduced and started to thicken. Season with salt and pepper. Divide the short ribs and vegetables between the serving plates and spoon 2 to 3 tablespoons of the sauce over each portion.

*Tip: When braising for long periods of time, you want to make sure you keep any vegetables going into the pot from being too small, as this will cause them to dry out.*

# French Onion Soup

*This recipe is great if you've got a surplus of onions and some day-old bread you'd like to use up.*

YIELD: **6 SERVINGS**

ACTIVE TIME: **30 MINUTES**

TOTAL TIME: **2 HOURS AND 30 MINUTES**

## INGREDIENTS

3 TABLESPOONS UNSALTED BUTTER

7 LARGE SWEET ONIONS, SLICED

2 TEASPOONS KOSHER SALT

⅓ CUP ORANGE JUICE

3 OZ. SHERRY

LEAVES FROM 3 SPRIGS FRESH THYME, FINELY CHOPPED

7 CUPS BEEF STOCK (SEE PAGE 15)

3 GARLIC CLOVES, MINCED

2 TEASPOONS BLACK PEPPER

6 SLICES DAY-OLD BREAD

1 CUP SHREDDED GRUYÈRE CHEESE

1 CUP SHREDDED EMMENTAL CHEESE

## DIRECTIONS

1. Place the butter, onions, and salt in a Dutch oven and cook over low heat while stirring often. Cook until the onions are dark brown and caramelized, 40 minutes to 1 hour.

2. Deglaze the pot with the orange juice and Sherry, using a wooden spoon to scrape any browned bits from the bottom of the pot.

3. Add the thyme, beef stock, and garlic, raise the heat to medium, and bring to a simmer. Simmer for 1 hour.

4. While the soup is simmering, preheat the oven to 450°F.

5. After 1 hour, ladle the soup into oven-safe bowls and place a slice of bread on top of each one. Divide the cheeses between the bowls, place them in the oven, and bake until the cheese begins to brown, about 10 to 15 minutes. Carefully remove the bowls from the oven and let cool for 10 minutes before serving.

# CHAPTER 4

# IN THE OVEN

---

*The considerable heat made available by the oven is another key tool to help you remain on top in the eternal struggle with complication. Once you get everything settled in a baking dish, you can simply set a timer, step away, and tend to another pressing matter—or relax with a beverage. Bouncing between vegetable-centered recipes that remain light while gaining in sweetness and texture to cheese-laden dishes that dissolve into decadent wonders, the preparations in this chapter will keep a smile on your face when the rest of the world—from the weather to work—are conspiring to do the opposite.*

YIELD: **4 TO 6 SERVINGS**

ACTIVE TIME: **15 MINUTES**

TOTAL TIME: **45 MINUTES**

# Chili-Dusted Cauliflower & Chickpea Salad

## INGREDIENTS

*Crunchy cauliflower, nutty chickpeas, and a perfect balance of sweet and spicy place this salad a cut above its peers.*

### FOR THE SALAD

1 (14 OZ.) CAN CHICKPEAS, DRAINED AND RINSED

3 CUPS CAULIFLOWER FLORETS

3 GARLIC CLOVES, SLICED THIN

1 SHALLOT, SLICED THIN

⅓ CUP OLIVE OIL

½ TEASPOON DARK CHILI POWDER

½ TEASPOON CHIPOTLE POWDER

½ TEASPOON BLACK PEPPER

½ TEASPOON ONION POWDER

½ TEASPOON GARLIC POWDER

¼ TEASPOON PAPRIKA

1 TABLESPOON KOSHER SALT

### FOR THE DRESSING

2 SCALLIONS, TRIMMED AND SLICED THIN

2 FRESNO CHILI PEPPERS, STEMMED, SEEDED, AND SLICED THIN

3 TABLESPOONS SUGAR

¼ CUP RED WINE VINEGAR

½ TEASPOON DARK CHILI POWDER

½ TEASPOON CHIPOTLE POWDER

½ TEASPOON BLACK PEPPER

½ TEASPOON ONION POWDER

½ TEASPOON GARLIC POWDER

¼ TEASPOON PAPRIKA

½ TABLESPOON KOSHER SALT

## DIRECTIONS

1. Preheat the oven to 400°F. To prepare the salad, place all of the ingredients in a mixing bowl and toss to coat. Place the mixture in a 9 x 13-inch baking pan, place the pan in the oven, and roast until the cauliflower is slightly charred and still crunchy, about 30 minutes. Remove from the oven and let the mixture cool slightly.

2. To prepare the dressing, place all of the ingredients in a large mixing bowl and stir until the sugar has dissolved. Place the cooked cauliflower-and-chickpea mixture in the bowl, toss to coat, and serve.

# Skillet Meatloaf with Bacon

YIELD: **6 SERVINGS**

ACTIVE TIME: **10 MINUTES**

TOTAL TIME: **1 HOUR**

*This dish is a standard in most American homes because it's good enough to eat every single day.*

## INGREDIENTS

1½ LBS. GROUND BEEF

½ LB. GROUND PORK

1 YELLOW ONION, MINCED

2 TEASPOONS GARLIC POWDER

1 CUP BREAD CRUMBS

¼ CUP WHOLE MILK

2 EGGS, LIGHTLY BEATEN

2 TABLESPOONS TOMATO PASTE

2 TABLESPOONS WORCESTERSHIRE SAUCE

2 TEASPOONS OLIVE OIL

8 SLICES BACON

## DIRECTIONS

1. Preheat the oven to 375°F. Place the beef, pork, onion, garlic powder, bread crumbs, milk, eggs, tomato paste, and Worcestershire sauce in a bowl and use a wooden spoon or your hands to work the mixture until thoroughly combined.

2. Coat a 10-inch cast-iron skillet with the olive oil. Place the meat mixture in the pan and form it into a rectangle. Lay four slices of the bacon lengthwise over the top and place the remaining four on top crosswise, weaving them together.

3. Place the skillet in the oven and bake for 45 minutes, until the bacon is very crispy and the meat is cooked through. Remove the meatloaf from the oven and let cool for 10 minutes before slicing.

# Caprese Chicken

YIELD: **6 SERVINGS**

ACTIVE TIME: **15 MINUTES**

TOTAL TIME: **45 MINUTES**

*By tossing a traditional caprese salad between layers of thinly sliced chicken breast, you transform a ho-hum set of ingredients into a dazzling dinner.*

## INGREDIENTS

1 GARLIC CLOVE, MINCED

1 TEASPOON DRIED OREGANO

1 TEASPOON GRANULATED GARLIC

SALT AND PEPPER, TO TASTE

2 TABLESPOONS OLIVE OIL

2 LBS. BONELESS, SKINLESS
CHICKEN BREASTS, HALVED
ALONG THEIR EQUATOR

2 LBS. PLUM TOMATOES, SLICED

1 LB. FRESH MOZZARELLA CHEESE,
SLICED

LEAVES FROM 1 BUNCH
FRESH BASIL

BALSAMIC GLAZE, FOR GARNISH

## DIRECTIONS

1. Preheat the oven to 375°F. Place the minced garlic, oregano, granulated garlic, salt, and pepper in a bowl and stir to combine. Place 1 tablespoon of the olive oil and the sliced chicken breasts in a bowl and toss to coat. Dredge the chicken breasts in the garlic-and-spice mixture and set aside.

2. Coat the bottom of a 12-inch cast-iron skillet with the remaining oil and warm over medium-high heat. Working in batches, sear the chicken breasts for 1 minute on each side.

3. When all of the chicken has been seared, place half of the breasts in an even layer on the bottom of the skillet. Top with two-thirds of the tomatoes and mozzarella and half of the basil leaves. Place the remaining chicken breasts on top and cover with the remaining tomatoes, mozzarella, and basil.

4. Place the skillet in the oven and cook until the interior temperature of the chicken breasts is 165°F, about 10 minutes. Remove the skillet from the oven and let rest for 10 minutes. Drizzle the balsamic glaze over the top and serve.

# Sweet & Spicy Roasted Barley

YIELD: **4 SERVINGS**

ACTIVE TIME: **10 MINUTES**

TOTAL TIME: **1 HOUR AND 30 MINUTES**

*This dish is light, sweet, spicy, and nutty. Considering how affordable all of the ingredients are, that's whole a lot of flavor for not very much money.*

## INGREDIENTS

5 CARROTS, PEELED AND CUT INTO 3-INCH PIECES

OLIVE OIL, TO TASTE

SALT AND PEPPER, TO TASTE

6 DRIED PASILLA PEPPERS

2¼ CUPS BOILING WATER

1 CUP PEARL BARLEY

1 RED ONION, MINCED

2 TABLESPOONS ADOBO SEASONING

1 TABLESPOON SUGAR

1 TABLESPOON CHILI POWDER

¼ CUP FINELY CHOPPED FRESH OREGANO

## DIRECTIONS

1. Preheat the oven to 375°F. Place the carrots in a 9 x 13-inch baking pan, drizzle the olive oil over them, and season with salt and pepper. Place in the oven and roast until the carrots are slightly soft to the touch, about 45 minutes.

2. While the carrots are cooking, open the Pasilla peppers and discard the seeds and stems. Place the peppers in a bowl, add the boiling water, and cover the bowl with aluminum foil.

3. When the carrots are cooked, remove the pan from the oven and add the remaining ingredients and the liquid the peppers have been soaking in. Chop the reconstituted peppers, add them to the pan, and spread the mixture so that the liquid is covering the barley. Cover the pan tightly with aluminum foil, place it in the oven, and bake until the barley is tender, about 45 minutes. Fluff with a fork and serve immediately.

YIELD: **6 SERVINGS**

ACTIVE TIME: **15 MINUTES**

TOTAL TIME: **24 HOURS**

# Jerk Chicken with Vegetables

## INGREDIENTS

**FOR THE MARINADE**

2 TABLESPOONS FRESH
THYME LEAVES

2 HABANERO PEPPERS, STEMMED
AND SEEDED TO TASTE

½ YELLOW ONION

½ CUP BROWN SUGAR

½ TABLESPOON CINNAMON

½ TEASPOON GROUND NUTMEG

1 TABLESPOON ALLSPICE

2-INCH PIECE FRESH GINGER,
PEELED AND MINCED

1 CUP OLIVE OIL

2 TABLESPOONS SOY SAUCE

1 SCALLION

1 TABLESPOON KOSHER SALT

1 TABLESPOON BLACK PEPPER

1 TABLESPOON RICE VINEGAR

**FOR THE CHICKEN & VEGETABLES**

5 LBS. BONE-IN, SKIN-ON CHICKEN
PIECES

3 RED BEETS, PEELED AND DICED

3 CARROTS, PEELED AND DICED

1 LARGE SWEET POTATO, PEELED
AND DICED

3 TURNIPS, PEELED AND DICED

¼ CUP OLIVE OIL

SALT AND PEPPER, TO TASTE

2 TABLESPOONS FINELY CHOPPED
FRESH THYME

*By substituting root vegetables for the rice and beans that are traditionally served with jerk chicken, you add some nutrition to this delicious dish.*

## DIRECTIONS

1. To prepare the marinade, place all of the ingredients in a blender and puree until smooth.

2. To begin preparations for the chicken and vegetables, place the chicken in a large baking pan, pour the marinade over the chicken, and refrigerate overnight.

3. Preheat the oven to 375°F. Place the vegetables, oil, salt, and pepper in an 9 x 13-inch baking pan and roast for 30 minutes. Remove, add the thyme, return the pan to the oven, and roast for an additional 25 minutes. While the vegetables are roasting, remove the chicken from the refrigerator and let it come to room temperature.

4. Remove the pan from the oven. Shake the chicken to remove any excess marinade and then place the chicken on top of the vegetables. Return the pan to the oven and roast for 45 to 50 minutes, until the interiors of thickest parts of the chicken reach 165°F. Remove the pan from the oven and serve immediately.

# Chicken & Tomatillo Casserole

YIELD: **6 SERVINGS**

ACTIVE TIME: **15 MINUTES**

TOTAL TIME: **24 HOURS**

*Packed with shredded chicken and tangy tomatillos, this is what lasagna might have been had it been created in the Southwest.*

## INGREDIENTS

**FOR THE MARINADE**

1 TOMATILLO, HUSKED, RINSED, AND HALVED

1 PLUM TOMATO, HALVED

2 GARLIC CLOVES

1 SHALLOT, HALVED

1 POBLANO PEPPER, STEMMED, SEEDED, AND HALVED

¼ CUP OLIVE OIL

1 TABLESPOON KOSHER SALT

1 TABLESPOON CUMIN

**FOR THE CASSEROLE**

2 LBS. BONELESS, SKINLESS CHICKEN BREASTS, SLICED THIN

2 EGGS, BEATEN

1 (14 OZ.) CAN FIRE-ROASTED TOMATOES

1 PINCH KOSHER SALT

14 CORN TORTILLAS

1 CUP SALSA VERDE (SEE PAGE 24)

¼ CUP CRUMBLED COTIJA CHEESE

## DIRECTIONS

1. To prepare the marinade, place all of the ingredients in a blender and puree until smooth.

2. To begin preparations for the casserole, place the chicken breasts in a large baking pan or resealable plastic bag. Pour the marinade over the chicken breasts and marinate in the refrigerator overnight.

3. Preheat the oven to 375°F. Place the chicken and marinade in a square 8-inch baking dish, place it in the oven, and roast until the center of the chicken reaches 165°F, about 30 minutes. Remove the dish from the oven, remove the chicken, transfer it to a mixing bowl, and shred it with a fork. Add the eggs, tomatoes, and salt to the bowl and stir to combine.

4. Place four of the tortillas in the baking dish. Add half of the chicken mixture, top with four more tortillas, and add the remaining chicken mixture. Top with remaining tortillas, cover with the Salsa Verde, and then place the dish in the oven. Bake for about 30 minutes, until the center is hot. Remove, sprinkle the cheese on top, and return to the oven. Bake until the cheese has melted, remove, and serve.

# Kibbeh bil Sanieh

YIELD: **4 SERVINGS**

ACTIVE TIME: **20 MINUTES**

TOTAL TIME: **1 HOUR AND 20 MINUTES**

*This deeply flavorful Levantine dish leans heavily on the smoky depth of Aleppo pepper, but if you can't track it down, red pepper flakes will do.*

## INGREDIENTS

2 TABLESPOONS OLIVE OIL

1 LARGE YELLOW ONION, MINCED

1½ LBS. GROUND BEEF

½ CUP PINE NUTS

2 TEASPOONS ALLSPICE

2 CUPS BULGUR WHEAT, RINSED

1 TABLESPOON TOMATO PASTE

1 TABLESPOON ALEPPO PEPPER

1 TABLESPOON KOSHER SALT, PLUS MORE TO TASTE

LEMON WEDGES, FOR SERVING

## DIRECTIONS

1. Preheat the oven to 350°F. Place half of the oil in a large skillet and warm over medium heat. When it is shimmering, add half of the onion and sauté until translucent, about 3 minutes. Add two-thirds of the ground beef and cook, breaking it up with a wooden spoon as it cooks, until lightly browned, about 8 minutes. Transfer the meat-and-onion mixture to a bowl, add the pine nuts and half of the allspice, and stir to combine. Set the mixture aside.

2. Place the remaining beef, onion, and allspice in a food processor with the bulgur, tomato paste, Aleppo pepper, and salt. Pulse until it is a paste.

3. Grease a 10-inch cast-iron skillet and cover the bottom of the pan with the meat-and-bulgur paste. Press down to create an even layer. Top with the meat-and-pine nut mixture and score it in a crosshatch pattern. Drizzle the remaining oil over the top and place the skillet in the oven. Bake for 1 hour, until the bulgur is tender. Remove from the oven, season with salt, and serve with the lemon wedges.

# Roasted Brussels Sprouts with Hot Honey & Hazelnuts

YIELD: **4 SERVINGS**

ACTIVE TIME: **10 MINUTES**

TOTAL TIME: **50 MINUTES**

*Don't be afraid to branch out into spicier peppers for the hot honey, as the sweetness of the honey balances the heat incredibly well.*

## INGREDIENTS

1½ LBS. BRUSSELS SPROUTS, TRIMMED AND HALVED

3 TABLESPOONS OLIVE OIL

SALT AND PEPPER, TO TASTE

½ CUP HOT HONEY (SEE SIDEBAR)

½ CUP CHOPPED HAZELNUTS

½ CUP GRATED PARMESAN CHEESE

## DIRECTIONS

1. Preheat the oven to 400°F. Place the Brussels sprouts in a bowl with the oil and salt and toss to combine. Transfer to a baking sheet, place it in the oven, and roast for 30 to 40 minutes, until the Brussels sprouts are well browned.

2. Remove the Brussels sprouts from the oven and let them cool slightly. Place them in a mixing bowl, add the Hot Honey, hazelnuts, and Parmesan, and toss to combine. Season with salt and pepper and serve.

---

### HOT HONEY

Place 4 hot chili peppers (Fresno and cayenne produce the best results) and 1 cup honey in a saucepan and bring to a very gentle simmer over medium-low heat. Reduce heat to lowest possible setting and cook for 1 hour. Remove the saucepan from heat and let the mixture infuse for another hour. Remove the peppers. Transfer the honey to an airtight container, cover, and store in the refrigerator.

# Roasted Asparagus with Sunny-Side Eggs & Lemon-Pepper Mayonnaise

YIELD: **6 SERVINGS**

ACTIVE TIME: **20 MINUTES**

TOTAL TIME: **35 MINUTES**

*For a cook, the most exciting thing about seeing flowers return in the spring is knowing that asparagus season is right around the corner.*

## INGREDIENTS

**FOR THE ASPARAGUS & EGGS**

SALT AND PEPPER, TO TASTE

2 BUNCHES ASPARAGUS, TRIMMED

2 TABLESPOONS OLIVE OIL

2 TABLESPOONS UNSALTED BUTTER

6 EGGS

3 TABLESPOONS PARMESAN CHEESE, GRATED, FOR GARNISH

**FOR THE MAYONNAISE**

1 CUP MAYONNAISE

ZEST AND JUICE OF 1 LEMON

½ TABLESPOON BLACK PEPPER

2 TEASPOONS KOSHER SALT

## DIRECTIONS

1. Preheat the oven to 400°F. To begin preparations for the asparagus and eggs, bring a large pot of salted water to a boil and prepare an ice water bath in a large bowl.

2. Place the asparagus in the boiling water and cook for 30 seconds. Drain and transfer to the ice water bath until it is completely cool, about 3 minutes. Transfer to a kitchen towel to dry completely.

3. To prepare the mayonnaise, place all of the ingredients in a mixing bowl and whisk to combine. Set aside.

4. Pat the asparagus dry. Place the olive oil in a skillet and warm over medium-high heat. Working in batches, add the asparagus when the oil starts to shimmer and cook until browned all over, about 4 minutes per batch. Transfer the cooked asparagus to a plate and tent with foil to keep warm.

5. Place the butter in a cast-iron skillet and melt over medium heat. Crack the eggs into the pan, taking care not to break the yolks. Season with salt and pepper and place the skillet in the oven. Bake until the whites are cooked through, 2 to 3 minutes. Remove from the oven.

6. To serve, spread some of the mayonnaise on a plate and lay some asparagus on top. Top each portion with an egg and garnish with the grated Parmesan.

# Pork & Apple Casserole

YIELD: **4 SERVINGS**

ACTIVE TIME: **10 MINUTES**

TOTAL TIME: **1 HOUR**

*A twist on the classic dinner of pork chops and applesauce, slow-roasted in the oven so that the pork remains at its most succulent.*

## INGREDIENTS

8 APPLES, CORED AND SLICED

2 TEASPOONS CINNAMON

1 TEASPOON GROUND NUTMEG

¼ CUP SUGAR

¼ CUP ALL-PURPOSE FLOUR

SALT AND PEPPER, TO TASTE

¼ CUP APPLE CIDER

1½-LB. PORK TENDERLOIN

2 TABLESPOONS GROUND
FRESH ROSEMARY

2 TABLESPOONS GROUND
FRESH THYME

## DIRECTIONS

1. Preheat the oven to 325°F. Place the apples, cinnamon, nutmeg, sugar, flour, and a pinch of salt in a mixing bowl and stir to combine. Transfer the mixture to a baking dish or Dutch oven and then add the apple cider.

2. Rub the pork tenderloin with the ground herbs and a pinch of salt. Place the pork on top of the apple mixture, cover, and place in the oven. Cook until a meat thermometer inserted into the center of the tenderloin registers 145°F, about 40 minutes.

3. Remove the pork tenderloin from the oven and slice. Serve on beds of the apple mixture.

# Creamy Curry Kuri Soup

YIELD: **6 SERVINGS**

ACTIVE TIME: **30 MINUTES**

TOTAL TIME: **2 HOURS**

*Kuri is a thin-skinned, orange squash with a flavor similar to chestnuts. It sounds exotic, but you can likely find it at your local farmers market.*

## INGREDIENTS

1 LARGE KURI SQUASH, QUARTERED

1 LARGE ONION, SLICED

2 TABLESPOONS OLIVE OIL

SALT AND PEPPER, TO TASTE

2 TABLESPOONS CURRY POWDER

4 TABLESPOONS UNSALTED BUTTER

1 CUP HEAVY CREAM

1 CUP WHOLE MILK

2 SPRIGS FRESH ROSEMARY

2 SPRIGS FRESH THYME

## DIRECTIONS

1. Preheat the oven to 400°F. Place the squash and onion in a baking dish, drizzle with the oil, and season with salt. Place the dish in the oven and cook until the onion has browned, 15 to 25 minutes. Remove the dish from the oven, transfer the onion to a bowl, return the squash to the oven, and cook until the flesh is tender, another 20 to 35 minutes. Remove the squash from the oven and let cool.

2. When the squash is cool enough to handle, scoop out the seeds. Scrape the flesh into the bowl containing the onion.

3. Place the squash, onion, and remaining ingredients in a large saucepan and bring to a boil over medium-high heat. Reduce heat to low and let the mixture simmer, while stirring occasionally, for 15 to 20 minutes.

4. Remove the thyme and rosemary sprigs. Transfer the soup to a blender and puree until desired texture is achieved. Season with salt and pepper and ladle into warmed bowls.

*Note: The toasted squash seeds will make for a lovely garnish for this soup. To take advantage of this, wash the seeds to remove any pulp and then pat them dry. Transfer them to a baking sheet, drizzle with olive oil, sprinkle with salt, and place the sheet in the oven. Bake for 5 minutes, remove them from the oven, and turn them over. Return to the oven and bake for another 5 minutes, until golden brown.*

# Five-Spice Turkey Breast

YIELD: **4 SERVINGS**

ACTIVE TIME: **15 MINUTES**

TOTAL TIME: **2 HOURS**

*Proof that turkey isn't just for the holidays, and doesn't need to be flanked by a number of rich sides.*

## INGREDIENTS

2 TABLESPOONS CHINESE FIVE-SPICE POWDER

1 TEASPOON CINNAMON

1 TABLESPOON BROWN SUGAR

1 TEASPOON BLACK PEPPER

1 BONE-IN, SKIN-ON WHOLE TURKEY BREAST

2 TABLESPOONS OLIVE OIL

## DIRECTIONS

1. Preheat the oven to 375°F. Place the five-spice powder, cinnamon, brown sugar, and pepper in a small bowl and stir to combine.

2. Pat the turkey breast dry with paper towels and coat it liberally with the spice mixture.

3. Place the oil in a 12-inch cast-iron skillet and warm over medium heat. When the oil starts to shimmer, add the turkey, skin-side down, and sear until it is browned, about 5 minutes.

4. Carefully turn the turkey over, cover the pan, and roast in the oven for 1½ hours.

5. Remove the pan from the oven and let the turkey rest for 15 minutes. Place the turkey breast on a cutting board, remove the bone, slice, and serve.

*Tip: You can also let the turkey cool down completely after removing it from the oven and make sandwiches on French bread with lots of shredded cabbage, carrots, and cilantro.*

# Roast Beef Au Jus with Vegetables

YIELD: **6 SERVINGS**

ACTIVE TIME: **25 MINUTES**

TOTAL TIME: **1 HOUR AND 30 MINUTES**

*The bright sweetness provided by the beets makes this dish perfect for those days when winter is beating you down.*

## INGREDIENTS

1 RED BEET, PEELED AND SLICED

1 CARROT, MINCED

1 PARSNIP, MINCED

2 CELERY STALKS, CHOPPED

1 YELLOW ONION, PEELED AND SLICED

1 ANAHEIM CHILI PEPPER, STEMMED, SEEDED, AND CHOPPED

3 GARLIC CLOVES, MINCED

1 TABLESPOON DRIED SAGE

1 TABLESPOON GRANULATED GARLIC

1 CUP BEEF STOCK (SEE PAGE 15)

1 CUP DRY RED WINE

2 TABLESPOONS WORCESTERSHIRE SAUCE

¼ CUP FINELY CHOPPED FRESH THYME

SALT AND PEPPER, TO TASTE

2-LB. EYE OF ROUND BEEF ROAST

2 TABLESPOONS OLIVE OIL

## DIRECTIONS

1. Preheat oven to 375°F. Place all of the ingredients, except for the roast, 2 tablespoons of the thyme, and the olive oil, in a 9 x 13-inch baking pan. Stir to evenly coat the vegetables.

2. Liberally coat the roast on all sides with the olive oil. Season with salt and pepper, sprinkle the remaining thyme on top, and then place the roast in the baking pan. Place the pan in the oven and cook until the center of the roast reads 120°F on an instant-read thermometer, about 40 to 45 minutes. Remove the pan from the oven and place the roast upside down on a cutting board. Cover with aluminum foil and let rest for 15 to 20 minutes before carving.

3. Use a slotted spoon to transfer the vegetables to a serving dish. Ladle the juices in the pan into a separate bowl.

4. Cutting against the grain, carve the meat into 1-inch-thick slices. Divide the vegetables between the plates and top with the slices of roast beef. Spoon the juices over the top and serve.

# CHAPTER 5

# MARINATE ON THAT

---

*The key to keeping your standards high and your interest engaged when marching toward minimalism is taking advantage of time and unique, quality ingredients. A marinade accomplishes both, allowing you to infuse your preparations with an unthinkable amount of flavor while requiring nothing more of you than the patience to let it sit and work its magic.*

# Quinoa & Black Bean Salad

YIELD: **4 TO 6 SERVINGS**

ACTIVE TIME: **25 MINUTES**

TOTAL TIME: **24 HOURS**

*Packed with flavor and high in protein, this is a guilt-free way to get a ton of nutrition without having to prepare a ton of different foods.*

## INGREDIENTS

2 CUPS WATER OR STOCK

1 CUP QUINOA, RINSED

1 LB. BLACK BEANS, SOAKED OVERNIGHT

1 CUP SALSA VERDE (SEE PAGE 24)

4 TOMATILLOS, HUSKED, RINSED, AND DICED

2 FRESNO CHILI PEPPERS, STEMMED, SEEDED, AND SLICED THIN

1 YELLOW BELL PEPPER, STEMMED, SEEDED, AND DICED

1 CUP BABY SPINACH

1 TABLESPOON KOSHER SALT

1 TABLESPOON CUMIN

1 TABLESPOON GARLIC POWDER

1 TABLESPOON DRIED OREGANO

## DIRECTIONS

1. Place the water or stock in a saucepan and bring to a boil. Add the quinoa, reduce heat to low, cover, and cook until tender, about 15 minutes.

2. Fluff the quinoa with a fork and transfer to a large salad bowl. Drain and rinse the beans, place them in the same saucepan used for the quinoa, and cover with water. Bring to a simmer and cook until the beans are fork-tender, about 1 hour.

3. While the beans are cooking, add the remaining ingredients to the salad bowl, stir to combine, and place the salad in the refrigerator until the beans are done cooking.

4. Drain and rinse beans under cold water until they are cool. Stir them into the salad and serve.

# Green Bean & Tofu Casserole

YIELD: **4 SERVINGS**

ACTIVE TIME: **5 MINUTES**

TOTAL TIME: **48 HOURS**

*Slow roasting is the key here, as it concentrates everything the tofu soaked up while marinating.*

## INGREDIENTS

**FOR THE MARINADE**

3 TABLESPOONS SOY SAUCE

2 TABLESPOONS RICE VINEGAR

1 TABLESPOON SESAME OIL

1 TABLESPOON HONEY

1 PINCH CINNAMON

1 PINCH BLACK PEPPER

**FOR THE CASSEROLE**

1 LB. EXTRA-FIRM TOFU, DRAINED AND CHOPPED

1 LB. GREEN BEANS

4 OZ. SHIITAKE MUSHROOMS, SLICED

2 TABLESPOONS SESAME OIL

1 TABLESPOON SOY SAUCE

2 TABLESPOONS SESAME SEEDS, FOR GARNISH

## DIRECTIONS

1. To prepare the marinade, place all of the ingredients in a small bowl and stir to combine.

2. To begin preparations for the casserole, place the marinade and the tofu in a resealable plastic bag, place it in the refrigerator, and let marinate for 2 days.

3. Preheat the oven to 375°F. Remove the cubes of tofu from the bag. Place the green beans, mushrooms, sesame oil, and soy sauce in the bag and shake until the vegetables are coated.

4. Line a 9 x 13-inch baking pan with parchment paper and place the tofu on it in an even layer. Place in the oven and roast for 35 minutes. Remove the pan, flip the cubes of tofu over, and push them to the edges of the pan. Add the green bean-and-mushroom mixture, return the pan to the oven, and roast for 15 minutes, or until the green beans are cooked to your preference. Remove the pan from the oven, garnish with the sesame seeds, and serve.

# Mojo Chicken

YIELD: **4 SERVINGS**

ACTIVE TIME: **30 MINUTES**

TOTAL TIME: **2 HOURS AND 30 MINUTES**

*This fiery, Cuban-inspired dish will wake up your family's taste buds every time.*

## INGREDIENTS

1 YELLOW ONION, CHOPPED

10 GARLIC CLOVES, PEELED AND TRIMMED

2 SCOTCH BONNET PEPPERS, STEMMED, SEEDED, AND CHOPPED

1 CUP FINELY CHOPPED FRESH CILANTRO

1 TEASPOON DRIED THYME

1 TABLESPOON CUMIN

½ TEASPOON ALLSPICE

1 CUP ORANGE JUICE

½ CUP FRESH LEMON JUICE

½ TEASPOON CITRIC ACID

ZEST AND JUICE OF 1 LIME

¼ CUP OLIVE OIL

SALT AND PEPPER, TO TASTE

2 LBS. BONELESS, SKINLESS CHICKEN BREASTS

## DIRECTIONS

1. Place all of the ingredients, except for the chicken, in a food processor or blender and puree until smooth. Reserve ½ cup of the marinade, pour the rest into a large resealable plastic bag, and add the chicken. Place in the refrigerator and marinate for 2 hours. If time allows, let the chicken marinate for up to 8 hours.

2. Remove the chicken from the refrigerator, remove it from the marinade, and pat dry. Preheat your gas or charcoal grill to medium-high heat.

3. When the grill is about 450°F, add the chicken and cook until both sides are charred and the breasts are cooked through, 4 to 5 minutes per side. The chicken breasts should be springy to the touch when ready. Transfer the chicken to a plate and let sit for 10 minutes.

4. Place the reserved marinade in a saucepan and simmer over medium heat until it starts to thicken, about 10 minutes. Spoon it over the chicken and serve immediately.

# Chicken Kebabs

YIELD: **4 SERVINGS**

ACTIVE TIME: **20 MINUTES**

TOTAL TIME: **3 HOURS**

*This recipe is simply one of the best, and easiest, ways to make the most of succulent chicken thighs.*

## INGREDIENTS

2 TABLESPOONS PAPRIKA

1 TEASPOON TURMERIC

1 TEASPOON ONION POWDER

1 TEASPOON GARLIC POWDER

1 TABLESPOON DRIED OREGANO

¼ CUP OLIVE OIL,
PLUS MORE AS NEEDED

2 TABLESPOONS WHITE WINE
VINEGAR

1 CUP PLAIN GREEK YOGURT

1 TEASPOON KOSHER SALT,
PLUS MORE TO TASTE

3 LBS. BONELESS, SKINLESS
CHICKEN THIGHS, CUT INTO
BITE-SIZED PIECES

BLACK PEPPER, TO TASTE

LEMON WEDGES, FOR SERVING

## DIRECTIONS

1. Place the paprika, turmeric, onion powder, garlic powder, oregano, olive oil, vinegar, yogurt, and salt in a large bowl and whisk to combine. Add the chicken pieces and stir until they are coated. Cover the bowl, place it in the refrigerator, and let the chicken marinate for at least 2 hours. If time allows, let the chicken marinate overnight.

2. Remove the chicken from the refrigerator and let it sit at room temperature for about 30 minutes.

3. Preheat your gas or charcoal grill to medium-high heat or place a cast-iron grill pan or skillet over medium-high heat and warm for 10 minutes. While the grill or the pan is heating up, thread the chicken onto skewers and season with salt and pepper.

4. Brush the grill or the pan with a light coating of olive oil and then add the chicken kebabs. Cook, turning occasionally, until the chicken is well browned and cooked through, approximately 10 minutes. Serve warm or at room temperature with the lemon wedges.

# Beef Shawarma

YIELD: **4 TO 6 SERVINGS**

ACTIVE TIME: **10 MINUTES**

TOTAL TIME: **2 HOURS AND 15 MINUTES**

*The secret ingredient in this dish is sumac, a popular spice in Middle Eastern cuisine that adds a beguiling sourness.*

## INGREDIENTS

3 LBS. SIRLOIN

6 TABLESPOONS OLIVE OIL

3 TABLESPOONS RED WINE VINEGAR

JUICE OF 2 LEMONS

2 TEASPOONS CINNAMON

2 TABLESPOONS CORIANDER

1 TABLESPOON BLACK PEPPER

1 TEASPOON CARDAMOM

1 TEASPOON GROUND CLOVES

½ TEASPOON MACE

1 PINCH GROUND NUTMEG

1 TABLESPOON GARLIC POWDER

2 YELLOW ONIONS, SLICED INTO THIN HALF-MOONS

SALT, TO TASTE

1 TEASPOON SUMAC POWDER

1 CUP PLAIN GREEK YOGURT, FOR SERVING

PITA BREAD, FOR SERVING

2 PERSIAN CUCUMBERS, DICED, FOR SERVING

2 ROMA TOMATOES, DICED, FOR SERVING

½ CUP FRESH MINT LEAVES, TORN, FOR SERVING

## DIRECTIONS

1. Place sirloin in the freezer for 30 minutes so that it will be easier to slice. After 30 minutes, use an extremely sharp knife to slice it as thin as possible.

2. Place the sirloin in a large mixing bowl. Add the olive oil, vinegar, lemon juice, cinnamon, coriander, pepper, cardamom, cloves, mace, nutmeg, and garlic powder and stir to combine. Place in the refrigerator and let it marinate for 1 hour. If time allows, let the beef marinate overnight.

3. Place the sliced onions in a baking dish and cover with water. Add a pinch of salt and several ice cubes. Place in the refrigerator for 30 minutes.

4. Remove the meat from the refrigerator and let it come to room temperature. Drain the onions, squeeze to remove as much liquid as possible, and place them in a bowl. Add the sumac powder and toss to coat. Set aside.

5. Warm a cast-iron grill pan over high heat. When it is warm, add the meat in batches and cook, while turning, until it is browned all over, about 4 minutes per batch. To serve, place a dollop of yogurt on a pita and top with some of the meat, onions, cucumbers, tomatoes, and mint leaves.

# Carne Asada

YIELD: **4 SERVINGS**

ACTIVE TIME: **20 MINUTES**

TOTAL TIME: **3 HOURS**

*Most people make this on the grill, but even direct flame cannot equal the power of a cast-iron skillet here.*

## INGREDIENTS

1 JALAPEÑO PEPPER, STEMMED, SEEDED, AND MINCED

3 GARLIC CLOVES, MINCED

½ CUP CHOPPED FRESH CILANTRO

¼ CUP OLIVE OIL, PLUS MORE AS NEEDED

JUICE OF 1 SMALL ORANGE

2 TABLESPOONS APPLE CIDER VINEGAR

2 TEASPOONS CAYENNE PEPPER

1 TEASPOON ANCHO CHILI POWDER

1 TEASPOON GARLIC POWDER

1 TEASPOON PAPRIKA

1 TEASPOON KOSHER SALT

1 TEASPOON CUMIN

1 TEASPOON DRIED OREGANO

¼ TEASPOON BLACK PEPPER

2 LBS. FLANK OR SKIRT STEAK, TRIMMED

CORN TORTILLAS, FOR SERVING

## DIRECTIONS

1. Place all of the ingredients, except for the steak and the tortillas, in a baking dish or a large resealable plastic bag and stir to combine. Add the steak, place it in the refrigerator, and let marinate for at least 2 hours. If time allows, marinate the steak overnight.

2. Approximately 30 minutes before you are going to cook the steak, remove it from the marinade, pat it dry, and let it come to room temperature.

3. Place a 12-inch cast-iron skillet over high heat and add enough oil to coat the bottom. When the oil starts to shimmer, add the steak and cook on each side for 4 minutes for medium-rare.

4. Remove the steak from the pan and let rest for 5 minutes before slicing it into thin strips, making sure to cut against the grain. Serve with corn tortillas and your favorite taco toppings.

# Crying Tiger Beef

YIELD: **4 SERVINGS**

ACTIVE TIME: **15 MINUTES**

TOTAL TIME: **45 MINUTES**

*Don't be thrown by the name—the only tears resulting from this dish are those of joy.*

## INGREDIENTS

2 LBS. FLANK STEAK

2 TABLESPOONS SOY SAUCE

1 TABLESPOON OYSTER SAUCE

1 TABLESPOON BROWN SUGAR, PLUS 1 TEASPOON

1 LARGE TOMATO, SEEDED AND DICED

⅓ CUP FRESH LIME JUICE

¼ CUP FISH SAUCE

2 TABLESPOONS FINELY CHOPPED FRESH CILANTRO, PLUS MORE FOR GARNISH

1½ TABLESPOONS TOASTED RICE POWDER (SEE SIDEBAR)

1 TABLESPOON RED PEPPER FLAKES

3 TABLESPOONS FINELY CHOPPED FRESH MINT, FOR GARNISH

3 TABLESPOONS FINELY CHOPPED FRESH BASIL, FOR GARNISH

## DIRECTIONS

1. Place the steak in a bowl and add the soy sauce, oyster sauce, and the 1 tablespoon of brown sugar. Stir to combine and then let the steak marinate for 30 minutes.

2. Place a cast-iron skillet over high heat and spray it with nonstick cooking spray. Add the steak and cook for 4 minutes per side for medium-rare. Transfer to a plate, tent loosely with aluminum foil, and let rest for 5 minutes before slicing into thin strips, making sure to cut against the grain.

3. Place the tomato, lime juice, fish sauce, remaining brown sugar, cilantro, Toasted Rice Powder, and red pepper flakes in a bowl and stir to combine. The powder won't dissolve, but will serve to bind the rest of the ingredients together. Divide the dipping sauce between the serving bowls. Top with the slices of beef and garnish each portion with additional cilantro, mint, and basil.

## TOASTED RICE POWDER

Warm a cast-iron skillet over medium-high heat. Add the ½ cup jasmine rice and toast until it starts to brown, about 4 minutes. Remove and grind into a fine powder using a mortar and pestle.

# Sichuan Cumin Beef

YIELD: **4 SERVINGS**

ACTIVE TIME: **10 MINUTES**

TOTAL TIME: **1 HOUR AND 15 MINUTES**

*This extremely fragrant recipe possesses equally heady flavors thanks to the unique buzz the Sichuan peppercorn supplies.*

## INGREDIENTS

3 TABLESPOONS CUMIN SEEDS

2 TEASPOONS SICHUAN PEPPERCORNS

1 TEASPOON KOSHER SALT

3 TABLESPOONS OLIVE OIL

4 WHOLE DRIED RED CHILI PEPPERS

2 TEASPOONS RED PEPPER FLAKES

1½ LBS. CHUCK STEAK, CUT INTO 1-INCH PIECES

1 YELLOW ONION, SLICED

2 SCALLIONS, TRIMMED AND SLICED THIN, FOR GARNISH

½ CUP FINELY CHOPPED FRESH CILANTRO, FOR GARNISH

1½ CUPS COOKED JASMINE RICE, FOR SERVING

## DIRECTIONS

1. Place the cumin seeds and Sichuan peppercorns in a dry skillet and toast over medium heat until they are fragrant, about 1 minute, making sure they do not burn. Remove and grind to a fine powder with a mortar and pestle.

2. Place the salt, 2 tablespoons of the oil, the dried chilies, red pepper flakes, and the toasted spice powder into a large bowl and stir to combine. Add the steak and toss until coated. Cover the bowl with a kitchen towel and let stand for 1 hour.

3. Warm a skillet over high heat until the pan is extremely hot. Add the remaining oil, swirl to coat, and then add the steak and onion. Cook, stirring occasionally, until the beef is browned all over and cooked through, about 10 minutes. Garnish with the scallions and cilantro and serve with the rice.

# Raspberry & Tomato Gazpacho

YIELD: **4 TO 6 SERVINGS**

ACTIVE TIME: **10 MINUTES**

TOTAL TIME: **24 HOURS**

*Roasting the tomatoes adds considerable depth to this dish, which would otherwise be overwhelmed by the sweet-and-tart flavor of the raspberries.*

## INGREDIENTS

2 TO 3 LARGE HEIRLOOM TOMATOES

1 CUP RASPBERRIES

2 GARLIC CLOVES

½ CUP PEELED AND DICED CUCUMBER

2 TEASPOONS FRESH LEMON JUICE

2 TABLESPOONS OLIVE OIL

1 RED BELL PEPPER, STEMMED, SEEDED, AND CHOPPED

SALT AND PEPPER, TO TASTE

FRESH MINT LEAVES, FOR GARNISH

HEAVY CREAM, FOR GARNISH (OPTIONAL)

## DIRECTIONS

1. Preheat the oven to 425°F. Place the tomatoes on a baking sheet and roast until they start to collapse and their skins start to blister, about 10 to 15 minutes. Remove from the oven and let cool slightly.

2. Place the tomatoes and all of the remaining ingredients, except for the garnishes, in a blender, puree until smooth, and refrigerate overnight.

3. When ready to serve, ladle the soup into bowls and garnish each portion with mint leaves and, if desired, approximately 1 tablespoon of heavy cream.

# Kimchi

YIELD: **4 CUPS**

ACTIVE TIME: **25 MINUTES**

TOTAL TIME: **3 TO 7 DAYS**

*Simple, flavorful, and versatile, kimchi is the perfect introduction to your new best friend: fermentation.*

## INGREDIENTS

1 HEAD NAPA CABBAGE,
CUT INTO STRIPS

½ CUP KOSHER SALT

2-INCH PIECE FRESH GINGER,
PEELED AND MINCED

3 GARLIC CLOVES, MINCED

1 TEASPOON SUGAR

5 TABLESPOONS RED PEPPER FLAKES

3 BUNCHES OF SCALLIONS,
TRIMMED AND SLICED

WATER, AS NEEDED

## DIRECTIONS

1. Place the cabbage and salt in a large bowl and stir to combine. Wash your hands, or put on gloves, and work the mixture with your hands, squeezing to remove as much liquid as possible from the cabbage. Let the mixture stand for 2 hours.

2. Add all of the remaining ingredients, except for the water, work the mixture with your hands until well combined, and squeeze to remove as much liquid as possible.

3. Transfer the mixture to a large mason jar and press down so it is tightly packed together. The liquid should be covering the mixture. If it is not, add water until the mixture is submerged.

4. Cover the jar and let the mixture sit at room temperature for 3 to 7 days, removing the lid daily to release the gas that has built up. Store in the refrigerator for up to 6 months.

# Spicy Pickles

YIELD: **12 CUPS**

ACTIVE TIME: **20 MINUTES**

TOTAL TIME: **3 HOURS**

*A refreshing and delicious preparation that makes for a perfect snack or side.*

## INGREDIENTS

1 LB. PICKLING CUCUMBERS, SLICED THIN

1 SMALL YELLOW ONION, SLICED THIN

½ RED BELL PEPPER, STEMMED, SEEDED, AND SLICED THIN

1 HABANERO PEPPER, STEMMED, SEEDED, AND SLICED THIN

1 GARLIC CLOVE, SLICED

1 CUP SUGAR

1 CUP APPLE CIDER VINEGAR

2 TEASPOONS MUSTARD SEEDS

½ TEASPOON TURMERIC

1 PINCH BLACK PEPPER

⅓ CUP CANNING & PICKLING SALT

## DIRECTIONS

1. Place the cucumbers, onion, peppers, and garlic in a large bowl and stir to combine.

2. Place the sugar, apple cider vinegar, mustard seeds, turmeric, and black pepper in a large saucepan and bring to a boil over medium-high heat, while stirring to dissolve the sugar.

3. Add the vegetables and the salt and return to a boil. Remove the pot from heat and let it cool slightly. Fill sterilized mason jars with the vegetables and cover with the brine. Let cool completely before sealing and placing in the refrigerator. The pickles will keep in the refrigerator for up to 2 weeks.

# Chicken Vindaloo

YIELD: **6 SERVINGS**

ACTIVE TIME: **15 MINUTES**

TOTAL TIME: **2 HOURS AND 30 MINUTES**

*A few words of advice: add as much cayenne pepper as you and your family can handle, as this beloved preparation improves as it gets spicier.*

## INGREDIENTS

1 TABLESPOON GARAM MASALA

1 TEASPOON TURMERIC

2 TEASPOONS SWEET PAPRIKA

1 TEASPOON MUSTARD POWDER

2 TABLESPOONS SUGAR

1 TEASPOON CUMIN

½ TEASPOON CAYENNE PEPPER, OR TO TASTE

½ CUP RED WINE VINEGAR

¼ CUP TOMATO PASTE

5 TABLESPOONS OLIVE OIL

3 LBS. CHICKEN PIECES

1 LARGE YELLOW ONION, SLICED

6 GARLIC CLOVES, MINCED

1-INCH PIECE FRESH GINGER, PEELED AND MINCED

1 (14 OZ.) CAN CHOPPED TOMATOES, DRAINED

FRESH CILANTRO, FINELY CHOPPED, FOR GARNISH

## DIRECTIONS

1. Place the garam masala, turmeric, paprika, mustard powder, sugar, cumin, cayenne pepper, vinegar, tomato paste, and 2 tablespoons of the olive oil in a mixing bowl and stir to combine. Add the chicken to the mixture, turn until the pieces are evenly coated, cover the bowl, and place it in the refrigerator for 2 hours. If time allows, let the chicken marinate overnight.

2. Place a Dutch oven over high heat and add the remaining oil. When the oil starts to shimmer, add the onion and cook until it is translucent, about 3 minutes. Reduce the heat to medium, add the garlic and ginger, and sauté for 1 minute.

3. Add the tomatoes, chicken, and the marinade to the pot and bring to a boil. Reduce the heat and simmer until the chicken is cooked through, about 18 minutes. Garnish with the cilantro and serve.

# CHAPTER 6

# WHAT'S
# LEFT

---

*A little bit of planning is a must if you are going to be successful in your attempt to simplify your life. An easy way to get accustomed to this reality is to turn what remains of your meal into the base of the next day's dinner. Saving time, helping you cut down considerably on waste, and transforming what would otherwise be the ho-hum, underwhelming contents of a Tupperware into a great dish, the recipes in this chapter will actually have you excited about the prospect of planning menus and plotting shopping lists.*

# Ham & Swiss Strata

YIELD: **4 SERVINGS**

ACTIVE TIME: **20 MINUTES**

TOTAL TIME: **1 HOUR**

*While this dish is the ideal way to use up leftovers, you can tell your guests you made it to showcase the flawless combination of ham and Emmental cheese.*

## INGREDIENTS

7 EGGS, BEATEN

2 CUPS WHOLE MILK

4 OZ. EMMENTAL CHEESE, SHREDDED

1 PINCH GROUND NUTMEG

3 CUPS DAY-OLD BREAD PIECES

1 CUP DICED LEFTOVER HAM

1 YELLOW ONION, MINCED

2 CUPS CHOPPED SPINACH

SALT AND PEPPER, TO TASTE

2 TEASPOONS OLIVE OIL

## DIRECTIONS

1. Place the eggs and milk in a large mixing bowl and whisk to combine. Add the cheese and nutmeg and stir to incorporate. Add the bread pieces, transfer the mixture to the refrigerator, and chill for 30 minutes.

2. Preheat the oven to 400°F. Add the ham, onion, and spinach to the egg-and-bread mixture and stir until evenly distributed. Season with salt and pepper.

3. Coat a 10-inch cast-iron skillet with the olive oil. Pour in the strata, place the skillet in the oven, and bake until it is golden brown and set in the center, about 25 minutes. Remove from the oven and let cool for 10 minutes before cutting into wedges and serving.

# Leftover Turkey Soup

YIELD: **4 SERVINGS**

ACTIVE TIME: **15 MINUTES**

TOTAL TIME: **40 MINUTES**

*Very little heavy lifting makes this a perfect dish for the Saturday after Thanksgiving.*

## INGREDIENTS

1 TABLESPOON OLIVE OIL

½ YELLOW ONION, MINCED

1 CARROT, PEELED AND MINCED

1 CELERY STALK, MINCED

1 TABLESPOON FINELY CHOPPED FRESH THYME

4 CUPS CHICKEN STOCK (SEE PAGE 12)

SALT AND PEPPER, TO TASTE

1½ CUPS EGG NOODLES

2 CUPS CHOPPED LEFTOVER TURKEY

## DIRECTIONS

1. Place the oil in a Dutch oven and warm over medium-high heat. When the oil starts to shimmer, add the onion and cook until it starts to soften, about 5 minutes. Add the carrot and celery, cook until tender, and then add the thyme and stock. Bring to a boil, reduce the heat, and simmer for 20 minutes.

2. Season the soup with salt and pepper, add the egg noodles and the turkey, and cook until the noodles are al dente, about 7 minutes. Ladle into warmed bowls and serve.

# Rice Bowl with Benihana's Ginger Dressing

YIELD: **4 SERVINGS**

ACTIVE TIME: **10 MINUTES**

TOTAL TIME: **20 MINUTES**

## INGREDIENTS

**FOR THE RICE BOWL**

1 TABLESPOON OLIVE OIL

1 LB. EXTRA-FIRM TOFU, DRAINED AND CHOPPED

2 CUPS DAY-OLD WHITE RICE, AT ROOM TEMPERATURE

2 CARROTS, PEELED AND GRATED

1 CUP BROCCOLI SPROUTS

1 CUP CORN KERNELS

1 CUP EDAMAME

FLESH FROM 2 AVOCADOS, SLICED THIN

SALT, TO TASTE

SESAME SEEDS, FOR GARNISH

**FOR THE DRESSING**

¼ CUP CHOPPED WHITE ONION

¼ CUP PEANUT OIL

1 TABLESPOON RICE VINEGAR

1-INCH PIECE FRESH GINGER, PEELED AND MINCED

1 TABLESPOON MINCED CELERY

1 TABLESPOON SOY SAUCE

1 TEASPOON TOMATO PASTE

1½ TEASPOONS SUGAR

1 TEASPOON FRESH LEMON JUICE

½ TEASPOON KOSHER SALT

*The restaurant chain's famed dressing lifts what should be a humble bowl of rice and vegetables.*

## DIRECTIONS

1. To begin preparations for the rice bowl, place the oil in a large skillet and warm over medium-high heat. When the oil starts to shimmer, add the tofu and cook until it is browned all over, turning the pieces as necessary.

2. To prepare the dressing, place all of the ingredients in a blender and puree until smooth.

3. Divide the rice between four bowls. Artfully arrange the tofu, carrots, broccoli sprouts, corn, edamame, and avocados on top of each portion.

4. Top each portion with a pinch of salt and the dressing, garnish with the sesame seeds, and serve.

# Curried Chicken Salad

YIELD: **6 SERVINGS**

ACTIVE TIME: **15 MINUTES**

TOTAL TIME: **20 MINUTES**

*If you're one of those doing all they can to avoid carbs, eschew the marble rye and serve this simple, flavor-packed salad over the baby arugula.*

## INGREDIENTS

4 CUPS DICED LEFTOVER CHICKEN

¼ CUP MAYONNAISE

3 TABLESPOONS FRESH LIME JUICE

¼ CUP MADRAS CURRY POWDER

1 TABLESPOON CUMIN

1 TABLESPOON GRANULATED GARLIC

½ TEASPOON CINNAMON

½ TEASPOON TURMERIC

SALT AND PEPPER, TO TASTE

3 CELERY STALKS, MINCED

2 GRANNY SMITH APPLES,
CORED AND MINCED

½ RED BELL PEPPER, STEMMED,
SEEDED, AND MINCED

¾ CUP PECANS, CHOPPED

6 OZ. BABY ARUGULA

12 SLICES MARBLE RYE, TOASTED

## DIRECTIONS

1. Place the chicken, mayonnaise, lime juice, and all of the seasonings in a mixing bowl and stir to combine. Add the celery, apples, red pepper, and ½ cup of the pecans and stir to incorporate.

2. Add the arugula and toss to combine. Top with the remaining pecans and make sandwiches with the toasted slices of marble rye.

# Chilled Corn Salad

YIELD: **4 SERVINGS**

ACTIVE TIME: **5 MINUTES**

TOTAL TIME: **3 HOURS AND 10 MINUTES**

*This recipe is a riff on a classic Mexican dish known as esquites, and it can easily be altered to suit your taste and the changing seasons.*

## INGREDIENTS

4 CUPS CORN KERNELS
(ABOUT 6 EARS OF CORN)

2 TABLESPOONS UNSALTED BUTTER

1 JALAPEŃO PEPPER, STEMMED,
SEEDED, AND DICED

2 TABLESPOONS MAYONNAISE

2 TEASPOONS GARLIC POWDER

3 TABLESPOONS SOUR CREAM

¼ TEASPOON CAYENNE PEPPER

¼ TEASPOON CHILI POWDER

2 TABLESPOONS FETA CHEESE

2 TABLESPOONS COTIJA CHEESE

2 TEASPOONS FRESH LIME JUICE

½ CUP FINELY CHOPPED FRESH
CILANTRO

SALT AND PEPPER, TO TASTE

4 CUPS LETTUCE OR ARUGULA

## DIRECTIONS

1. Place all of the ingredients, except for the lettuce or arugula, in a large mixing bowl and stir to combine.

2. Chill the salad in the refrigerator for 3 hours. When ready to serve, add the lettuce or arugula and stir to incorporate.

# Panzanella with White Balsamic Vinaigrette

YIELD: **6 SERVINGS**

ACTIVE TIME: **15 MINUTES**

TOTAL TIME: **15 MINUTES**

*When caught in the breakneck pace of the summer, quick dishes that can salvage ingredients that have lingered slightly too long are extremely valuable. This salad is one such treasure.*

## INGREDIENTS

**FOR THE SALAD**

1 TABLESPOON KOSHER SALT, PLUS 2 TEASPOONS

6 PEARL ONIONS, TRIMMED

1 CUP CORN KERNELS

1 CUP CHOPPED GREEN BEANS

4 CUPS CHOPPED DAY-OLD BREAD

2 CUPS CHOPPED OVERRIPE TOMATOES

10 LARGE FRESH BASIL LEAVES, TORN

BLACK PEPPER, TO TASTE

**FOR THE VINAIGRETTE**

½ CUP WHITE BALSAMIC VINEGAR

¼ CUP OLIVE OIL

2 TABLESPOONS MINCED SHALLOT

¼ CUP SLICED SCALLIONS

2 TABLESPOONS FINELY CHOPPED FRESH PARSLEY

2 TEASPOONS KOSHER SALT

1 TEASPOON BLACK PEPPER

## DIRECTIONS

1. To begin preparations for the salad, bring water to a boil in a small saucepan and prepare an ice water bath. When the water is boiling, add the tablespoon of salt and the pearl onions and cook for 5 minutes. When the onions have 1 minute left to cook, add the corn and green beans to the saucepan. Transfer the vegetables to the ice water bath and let cool completely.

2. Remove the pearl onions from the ice water bath and squeeze to remove the bulbs from their skins. Cut the bulbs in half and break them down into individual petals. Drain the corn and green beans and pat the vegetables dry.

3. To prepare the vinaigrette, place all of the ingredients in a mixing bowl and whisk until combined.

4. Place the cooked vegetables, bread, tomatoes, and basil in a salad bowl and toss to combine. Add the remaining salt, season with pepper, and add half of the vinaigrette. Toss to coat, taste, and add more of the vinaigrette if desired.

# Thai Beef & Cucumber Salad

YIELD: **2 SERVINGS**

ACTIVE TIME: **15 MINUTES**

TOTAL TIME: **1 HOUR AND 30 MINUTES**

## INGREDIENTS

2 OZ. THIN RICE NOODLES

1 CARROT, PEELED AND GRATED

1 SMALL CUCUMBER,
SEEDED AND DICED

JUICE AND ZEST OF 1 LIME

10 FRESH MINT LEAVES, CHOPPED

1 TO 2 TABLESPOONS SOY SAUCE

1 TEASPOON REAL MAPLE SYRUP

½ TEASPOON KOSHER SALT

1 TABLESPOON FISH SAUCE

1 CUP CHOPPED LEFTOVER ROAST
BEEF OR STEAK

RICE VINEGAR, TO TASTE

HOT SAUCE, TO TASTE

*This is a light but filling salad, and is a perfect use for leftover roast beef or steak. The whole recipe requires no cooking save boiling water for the noodles.*

## DIRECTIONS

1. Bring 6 cups of water to a boil in a medium saucepan and place the noodles in a baking dish. Pour the water over the noodles and let sit until tender, about 20 minutes. Drain well and place them in a bowl.

2. Add the remaining ingredients and toss to combine. Chill in the refrigerator for 1 hour and serve.

# Pork Fried Rice

---

*If you learn how to plan properly, the leftover pork and rice from one night can set you up perfectly for this dish.*

YIELD: **8 SERVINGS**

ACTIVE TIME: **15 MINUTES**

TOTAL TIME: **25 MINUTES**

## INGREDIENTS

¼ CUP OLIVE OIL

1-INCH PIECE FRESH GINGER, PEELED AND MINCED

2 GARLIC CLOVES, MINCED

3 LARGE EGGS

2 CUPS MINCED CARROTS

4 CUPS DAY-OLD WHITE RICE

4 SCALLIONS, TRIMMED AND CHOPPED

1 CUP PEAS

2 TABLESPOONS SOY SAUCE

1 TABLESPOON RICE VINEGAR

1 TABLESPOON FISH SAUCE

1 TABLESPOON SESAME OIL

2 CUPS CHOPPED LEFTOVER PORK TENDERLOIN

## DIRECTIONS

1. Place the oil in a 12-inch cast-iron skillet and warm over medium-high heat. When the oil starts to shimmer, add the ginger and garlic and cook until they just start to brown, about 2 minutes.

2. Add the eggs and scramble until they are set, about 2 minutes. Add the carrots, rice, scallions, and peas and stir to incorporate. Add the soy sauce, rice vinegar, fish sauce, sesame oil, and pork and cook, while stirring constantly, until everything is heated through, about 5 minutes. Serve immediately.

# Lamb & Sweet Potato Hash

YIELD: **4 TO 6 SERVINGS**

ACTIVE TIME: **20 MINUTES**

TOTAL TIME: **30 MINUTES**

*If you really want to take this dish to the next level, fry an egg and place it on top of each portion.*

## INGREDIENTS

1 LB. SWEET POTATOES, PEELED AND MINCED

2 TABLESPOONS CLARIFIED UNSALTED BUTTER

2 POBLANO PEPPERS, STEMMED, SEEDED, AND DICED

2 YELLOW ONIONS, MINCED

2 GARLIC CLOVES, MINCED

1 TABLESPOON CUMIN

3 CUPS CHOPPED LEFTOVER LAMB

1 TABLESPOON KOSHER SALT, PLUS MORE TO TASTE

1 TABLESPOON FINELY CHOPPED FRESH OREGANO

BLACK PEPPER, TO TASTE

## DIRECTIONS

1. Fill a 12-inch cast-iron skillet with water and bring to a boil. Add the sweet potatoes and cook until they are just tender, about 7 minutes. Be careful not to overcook them, as you don't want to end up with mashed potatoes in the hash. Drain the potatoes and set aside.

2. Add the clarified butter, poblano peppers, onions, garlic, and cumin to the skillet and cook over medium heat until all of the vegetables are soft, about 10 minutes.

3. Add the lamb and return the potatoes to the skillet. Add the salt and cook until everything is warmed through, another 5 minutes. Add the oregano, stir to incorporate, season with pepper, and serve.

# Avgolemono

YIELD: **4 SERVINGS**

ACTIVE TIME: **10 MINUTES**

TOTAL TIME: **20 MINUTES**

*One of the most popular soups in Greek cuisine, it roughly translates to "egg and lemon," and these two ingredients combine to produce a nourishing soup that is still nice and light.*

## INGREDIENTS

6 CUPS CHICKEN STOCK
(SEE PAGE 12)

½ CUP ORZO

3 EGGS

1 TABLESPOON FRESH LEMON JUICE

1 TABLESPOON COLD WATER

1½ CUPS CHOPPED LEFTOVER
CHICKEN

SALT AND PEPPER, TO TASTE

LEMON SLICES, FOR GARNISH

FRESH PARSLEY, FINELY CHOPPED,
FOR GARNISH

## DIRECTIONS

1. Place the stock in a large saucepan and bring to a boil. Reduce heat so that the stock simmers. Add the orzo and cook until tender, about 5 minutes.

2. Strain the stock and orzo over a large bowl. Set the orzo aside. Return the stock to the pan and bring to a simmer.

3. Place the eggs in a mixing bowl and beat until frothy. Add the lemon juice and cold water and whisk to incorporate. While stirring constantly, add approximately ½ cup of the stock to the mixture. Stir another cup of stock into the egg mixture and then add the tempered eggs to the saucepan. Be careful not to let the stock come to a boil once you add the tempered eggs.

4. Add the chicken and return the orzo to the soup. Cook, while stirring, until everything is warmed through, about 5 minutes. Season with salt and pepper, ladle into warmed bowls, and garnish with the lemon slices and parsley.

# Garden Sesame Noodles

YIELD: **6 SERVINGS**

ACTIVE TIME: **15 MINUTES**

TOTAL TIME: **30 MINUTES**

*A great recipe for cucumbers and everything else out of a summer garden.*

## INGREDIENTS

1 LB. CHINESE EGG NOODLES

3 TABLESPOONS TOASTED SESAME OIL

2 TABLESPOONS TAHINI

1½ TABLESPOONS SMOOTH PEANUT BUTTER

¼ CUP SOY SAUCE

2 TABLESPOONS RICE VINEGAR

1 TABLESPOON LIGHT BROWN SUGAR

2 TEASPOONS CHILI GARLIC SAUCE, PLUS MORE FOR SERVING

2-INCH PIECE GINGER, PEELED AND GRATED OR MINCED

2 GARLIC CLOVES, MINCED

1 YELLOW OR ORANGE BELL PEPPER, STEMMED, SEEDED, AND SLICED THIN

2 CUPS CHOPPED LEFTOVER CHICKEN

1 CUCUMBER, PEELED, SEEDED, AND SLICED THIN

1 CUP SNOW PEAS, TRIMMED

½ CUP CHOPPED ROASTED PEANUTS

2 TABLESPOONS SESAME SEEDS, TOASTED

6 SCALLIONS, TRIMMED AND CHOPPED

## DIRECTIONS

1. Bring a large pot of water to a boil. Add the noodles and stir for the first minute to prevent any sticking. Cook until tender but still chewy, 2 to 3 minutes. Drain and transfer the noodles to a large bowl. Add ½ tablespoon of the sesame oil and toss to coat to prevent the noodles from sticking together.

2. Place the tahini and peanut butter in a small bowl. Add the soy sauce, vinegar, the remaining sesame oil, the sugar, chili garlic sauce, ginger, and garlic and whisk until combined. Taste and adjust the seasoning according to your preference.

3. Add the sauce to the noodles and toss until evenly distributed. Divide the noodles between six bowls and top with the pepper, chicken, cucumber, snow peas, peanuts, sesame seeds, and scallions. Serve with additional chili garlic sauce.

# Chicken & Coconut with Cucumber Noodles

YIELD: **4 SERVINGS**

ACTIVE TIME: **10 MINUTES**

TOTAL TIME: **40 MINUTES**

*The combination of warming, pungent cumin, sweet and soothing coconut, and crispy cucumber is endlessly satisfying.*

## INGREDIENTS

5 LARGE CUCUMBERS, PEELED, HALVED LENGTHWISE, AND SEEDED

½ CUP SHREDDED UNSWEETENED COCONUT

ZEST AND JUICE FROM 2 LIMES

¼ CUP COCONUT MILK

1 TEASPOON CHILI GARLIC SAUCE, PLUS MORE AS NEEDED

½-INCH PIECE FRESH GINGER, PEELED AND GRATED

1 TEASPOON SUGAR

1 TEASPOON CUMIN

1 TEASPOON KOSHER SALT, PLUS MORE TO TASTE

3 CUPS SHREDDED LEFTOVER CHICKEN

½ CUP ROASTED PEANUTS, CHOPPED, FOR GARNISH

6 SCALLIONS, TRIMMED AND SLICED THIN, FOR GARNISH

## DIRECTIONS

1. Quarter each cucumber half and then cut the quarters into ⅛-inch-wide "noodles." Place the strands on paper towels to drain for 30 minutes.

2. Place the coconut, lime juice, coconut milk, chili garlic sauce, ginger, sugar, cumin, and salt in a small food processor or a blender and puree until smooth.

3. Place the cucumber noodles and chicken in a large serving bowl. Top with the coconut mixture and toss to coat.

4. Sprinkle the lime zest, peanuts, and scallions on top of the dressed noodles, season to taste, and serve immediately.

# Pad Thai

YIELD: **4 TO 6 SERVINGS**

ACTIVE TIME: **10 MINUTES**

TOTAL TIME: **20 MINUTES**

*The key here is balancing the flavors properly so that you have a tangle of chewy noodles freighted with a delicious jumble of salty, sweet, sour, and spicy.*

## INGREDIENTS

6 OZ. WIDE RICE NOODLES

1 TABLESPOON OLIVE OIL

1 LARGE EGG

3 CUPS SHREDDED LEFTOVER CHICKEN

¼ CUP TAMARIND PASTE

2 TABLESPOONS WATER

1½ TABLESPOONS FISH SAUCE

2 TABLESPOONS RICE VINEGAR

1½ TABLESPOONS BROWN SUGAR

4 SCALLIONS, TRIMMED AND SLICED

1 CUP BEAN SPROUTS

½ TEASPOON CAYENNE PEPPER

¼ CUP CRUSHED PEANUTS

LIME WEDGES, FOR SERVING

## DIRECTIONS

1. Place the noodles in a baking dish and cover with boiling water. Stir and let stand until they are tender, about 15 minutes.

2. Place the oil in a large wok or skillet and warm over medium-high heat. When the oil starts to shimmer, add the egg and cook until it is almost set. Add the noodles and chicken and stir to incorporate. While stirring to incorporate with every addition, add the tamarind paste, water, fish sauce, vinegar, brown sugar, scallions, bean sprouts, cayenne pepper, and peanuts. Cook until everything is warmed through and serve with the lime wedges.

# Chicken Paninis with Sun-Dried Tomato Aioli

YIELD: **4 SERVINGS**

ACTIVE TIME: **10 MINUTES**

TOTAL TIME: **10 MINUTES**

*Constructing a delicious sandwich starts with quality bread. Once you've got that in place, the rest is easy.*

## INGREDIENTS

**FOR THE AIOLI**

1 CUP CHOPPED SUN-DRIED TOMATOES

1 CUP MAYONNAISE

1 TABLESPOON WHOLE GRAIN MUSTARD

2 TABLESPOONS FINELY CHOPPED FRESH PARSLEY

2 TABLESPOONS MINCED SCALLIONS

1 TEASPOON WHITE BALSAMIC VINEGAR

1 GARLIC CLOVE, MINCED

2 TEASPOONS KOSHER SALT

1 TEASPOON BLACK PEPPER

**FOR THE SANDWICHES**

8 SLICES SOURDOUGH BREAD

8 SLICES CHEDDAR CHEESE

4 LEFTOVER CHICKEN BREASTS, SLICED

12 SLICES COOKED BACON

1 CUP ARUGULA

## DIRECTIONS

1. Preheat a panini press. To prepare the aioli, place all of the ingredients in a mixing bowl and stir until combined.

2. To begin preparations for the sandwiches, spread some of the aioli on each slice of bread. Place a slice of cheddar on each slice of bread. Divide the chicken between four pieces of the bread. Top each portion of chicken with 3 slices of bacon and ¼ cup of the arugula. Assemble the sandwiches with the other slices of bread.

3. Place the sandwiches in the panini press and press until the cheese has melted and there is a nicely browned crust on the bread. Remove and serve immediately.

*Note: If you don't have a panini press, don't worry. Simply place 1 tablespoon of olive oil in a large skillet and warm over medium-high heat. Place a sandwich in the pan, place a cast-iron skillet on top so it is pressing down on the sandwich, and cook until golden brown. Turn the sandwich over and repeat.*

# CHAPTER 7

# SWEET

# CRAVINGS

---

*Since you've succeeded in your attempt to reduce complication in the kitchen, you deserve a little treat. But there's no reason to undo all the progress you've made and give back the time you've saved in procuring that indulgence. These desserts are straightforward, but possess flavors and appearances that belie their humble assembly, qualities that make them fitting realizations of those dreams you had of everything that simplifying your life could provide.*

# Chocolate Chip Cookies

YIELD: **16 COOKIES**

ACTIVE TIME: **15 MINUTES**

TOTAL TIME: **45 MINUTES**

*Browning the butter before incorporating it into the dough gives these classic cookies unparalleled flavor.*

## INGREDIENTS

14 TABLESPOONS UNSALTED BUTTER

1¾ CUPS ALL-PURPOSE FLOUR

½ TEASPOON BAKING SODA

½ CUP GRANULATED SUGAR

¾ CUP FIRMLY PACKED
DARK BROWN SUGAR

1 TEASPOON KOSHER SALT

2 TEASPOONS PURE
VANILLA EXTRACT

1 LARGE EGG

1 LARGE EGG YOLK

1¼ CUPS SEMISWEET
CHOCOLATE CHIPS

## DIRECTIONS

1. Preheat the oven to 350°F. Place the butter in a saucepan and cook over medium-high heat until it is dark brown and has a nutty aroma. Transfer to a heatproof mixing bowl.

2. Place the flour and baking soda in another mixing bowl and whisk until combined.

3. Add the sugars, salt, and vanilla to the bowl containing the melted butter and whisk until combined. Add the egg and egg yolk and whisk until mixture is smooth and thick. Add the flour-and-baking soda mixture and stir until incorporated. Add the chocolate chips and stir until evenly distributed. Form the mixture into 16 balls and place on parchment-lined baking sheets, leaving about 2 inches between each ball.

4. Working with one baking sheet at a time, place it in the oven and bake for about 12 minutes, rotating the sheet halfway through the bake time, until the edges are set and the cookies are golden brown. Remove from the oven and let cool on the baking sheets.

# Dark Chocolate & Stout Brownies

YIELD: **16 BROWNIES**

ACTIVE TIME: **15 MINUTES**

TOTAL TIME: **1 HOUR AND 15 MINUTES**

*Adding a rich, creamy stout to the brownie batter results in a perfectly moist brownie.*

## INGREDIENTS

12 OZ. GUINNESS OR OTHER STOUT

¾ LB. DARK CHOCOLATE CHIPS

2 STICKS UNSALTED BUTTER

1½ CUPS GRANULATED SUGAR

3 LARGE EGGS

1 TEASPOON PURE VANILLA EXTRACT

¾ CUP ALL-PURPOSE FLOUR

1¼ TEASPOONS KOSHER SALT

COCOA POWDER, FOR DUSTING

## DIRECTIONS

1. Preheat your oven to 350°F and grease a square 8-inch cake pan. Place the stout in a medium saucepan and bring to a boil. Cook until it has reduced by half. Remove the pan from heat and let cool completely.

2. Place the chocolate chips and the butter in a microwave-safe bowl and microwave on medium until melted, removing to stir every 15 seconds.

3. Place the sugar, eggs, and vanilla in a large bowl and stir until combined. Slowly whisk in the chocolate-and-butter mixture and then whisk in the stout.

4. Fold in the flour and salt. Pour the batter into greased pan, place it in oven, and bake for 35 to 40 minutes, until the surface begins to crack and a toothpick inserted in the center comes out with a few moist crumbs attached. Remove the pan from the oven, place on a wire rack, and let cool for at least 20 minutes. When cool, sprinkle the cocoa powder over the top and cut the brownies into squares.

# Chocolate Mousse

YIELD: **6 SERVINGS**

ACTIVE TIME: **10 MINUTES**

TOTAL TIME: **1 HOUR AND 10 MINUTES**

*Keep a lid on how simple this is to prepare—it's so good, no one will believe you anyway.*

## INGREDIENTS

1 CUP BITTERSWEET CHOCOLATE CHIPS

2 CUPS HEAVY CREAM, CHILLED

2 TABLESPOONS GRANULATED SUGAR

3 EGG WHITES

½ TEASPOON PURE VANILLA EXTRACT

¼ TEASPOON KOSHER SALT

WHIPPED CREAM, FOR SERVING

## DIRECTIONS

1. Place the chocolate chips in a microwave-safe bowl and microwave on medium until melted, removing to stir every 15 seconds.

2. Place the cream in a mixing bowl and beat until soft peaks form. Place the sugar, egg whites, vanilla, and salt in a separate bowl and beat until soft peaks form.

3. Gradually add the chocolate to the egg white mixture and stir until almost completely combined. Gently fold in the cream.

4. Transfer the mousse into the serving dishes and refrigerate for at least 1 hour. Top each serving with whipped cream.

## PASTRY CREAM

Place 2 cups whole milk and 1 tablespoon unsalted butter in a saucepan and bring to a simmer over medium heat. As the mixture is coming to a simmer, place ½ cup granulated sugar and 3 tablespoons cornstarch in a small bowl and whisk to combine. Add 2 large eggs and whisk until the mixture is smooth and creamy. While stirring constantly, gradually incorporate half of the milk mixture into the egg mixture. Add a pinch of kosher salt and ½ teaspoon of pure vanilla extract, stir to incorporate, and pour the tempered eggs into the saucepan. Cook, while stirring constantly, until the mixture is thick enough to coat the back of a wooden spoon, making sure not to let it come to a boil. Pour the cream into a bowl, place plastic wrap directly on the surface to prevent a skin from forming, and refrigerate until cool.

# Mille-Feuille

YIELD: **4 TO 6 SERVINGS**

ACTIVE TIME: **20 MINUTES**

TOTAL TIME: **45 MINUTES**

*You'll find no shortage of uses for the Pastry Cream that holds this aesthetically pleasing dessert together.*

## INGREDIENTS

2 SHEETS FROZEN PUFF PASTRY, THAWED

CONFECTIONERS' SUGAR, FOR DUSTING

PASTRY CREAM (SEE SIDEBAR)

ZEST OF 1 ORANGE

1 TABLESPOON GRAND MARNIER

1 PINT FRESH RASPBERRIES

## DIRECTIONS

1. Preheat the oven to 400°F. Roll out the sheets of puff pastry and place each one on a greased baking sheet. Dust with confectioners' sugar, place them in the oven, and bake for 12 to 15 minutes, until golden brown. Remove from the oven, transfer to a wire rack, and let cool.

2. Place the Pastry Cream in a bowl, add the orange zest and Grand Marnier, and fold to incorporate. Transfer the mixture into a piping bag fitted with a plain tip and place it in the refrigerator to chill while the puff pastry continues to cool.

3. Divide each sheet of the cooled puff pastry into 3 equal portions. Remove the piping bag from the freezer and place a thick layer of cream on one of the pieces of puff pastry. Dot the edges of the cream with the raspberries and press down on them gently. Fill the space between the raspberries with more of the cream and place another piece of puff pastry on top. Repeat the process with the cream and raspberries and then place the last piece of puff pastry on top. Carefully cut into the desired number of portions and serve.

# Vanilla Bread Pudding

YIELD: **4 TO 6 SERVINGS**

ACTIVE TIME: **20 MINUTES**

TOTAL TIME: **1 HOUR AND 45 MINUTES**

*A perfect spot for the rest of that baguette you brought home yesterday.*

## INGREDIENTS

2 TABLESPOONS UNSALTED BUTTER

8 CUPS DAY-OLD BAGUETTE PIECES

2 EGGS

1 TABLESPOON PURE VANILLA EXTRACT

2 CUPS HEAVY CREAM

2 CUPS WHOLE MILK

## DIRECTIONS

1. Place a cast-iron skillet over low heat and add the butter. When it is melted, add the baguette pieces and shake the skillet until they are coated. Transfer the pieces of bread into a large baking dish.

2. Place the eggs and vanilla extract in a mixing bowl and whisk until combined. Add the cream and milk and stir until just combined. Pour the mixture over the bread and shake the baking dish to evenly distribute. Cover the dish with aluminum foil and let stand in a cool place for 30 minutes. Preheat the oven to 350°F.

3. Remove the foil, place the dish in the oven, and bake until the pudding is set and browned at the edges, about 45 minutes. Remove from the oven and let cool for 5 to 10 minutes before transferring to a serving dish.

# Honey Nut Truffles

YIELD: **16 TO 20 TRUFFLES**

ACTIVE TIME: **10 MINUTES**

TOTAL TIME: **2 HOURS**

*Adding a bit of honey to the great combination of chocolate and peanut butter makes for an unforgettable bite.*

## INGREDIENTS

½ CUP PEANUT BUTTER

¼ CUP HONEY

¼ TEASPOON KOSHER SALT

1 CUP SEMISWEET CHOCOLATE CHIPS

## DIRECTIONS

1. Place the peanut butter, honey, and salt in a bowl and stir until well combined. Place teaspoon-sized balls of the mixture on a parchment-lined baking sheet and then place in the refrigerator for 1 hour.

2. Remove the baking sheet from the refrigerator. Place the chocolate chips in a microwave-safe bowl and microwave on medium until melted, removing to stir every 15 seconds.

3. Dip the balls into the melted chocolate until completely covered. Place them back on the baking sheet. When all of the truffles have been coated, refrigerate until the chocolate is set.

# Muddy Buddies

YIELD: **8 TO 10 SERVINGS**

ACTIVE TIME: **5 MINUTES**

TOTAL TIME: **50 MINUTES**

*So good you won't care that you end up covered in confectioners' sugar.*

## INGREDIENTS

1 CUP SEMISWEET CHOCOLATE CHIPS

¾ CUP CREAMY PEANUT BUTTER

1 TEASPOON PURE VANILLA EXTRACT

9 CUPS RICE CHEX

1½ CUPS CONFECTIONERS' SUGAR

## DIRECTIONS

1. Place the chocolate chips and peanut butter in a microwave-safe bowl and microwave on medium for 30 seconds. Remove from the microwave, add the vanilla, and stir until the mixture is smooth.

2. Place the Chex in a large mixing bowl and pour the peanut butter-and-chocolate mixture over the cereal. Carefully stir until all of the Chex are coated.

3. Place the mixture into a large resealable plastic bag and add the confectioners' sugar. Seal the bag and shake until each piece of Chex is coated with sugar.

4. Pour the mixture onto a parchment-lined baking sheet and refrigerate for 45 minutes before serving.

# Cherry Clafoutis

*Opinion is divided on whether to leave the pits in the cherries or remove them, but Julia Child—who introduced this recipe to the wider world—left them in, believing that they added considerable depth to the flavor.*

YIELD: **4 TO 6 SERVINGS**

ACTIVE TIME: **20 MINUTES**

TOTAL TIME: **45 MINUTES**

## INGREDIENTS

1 STICK UNSALTED BUTTER, MELTED

1 CUP GRANULATED SUGAR, PLUS 2 TEASPOONS

⅔ CUP ALL-PURPOSE FLOUR

½ TEASPOON KOSHER SALT

1 TEASPOON PURE VANILLA EXTRACT

3 EGGS, BEATEN

1 CUP WHOLE MILK

3 CUPS CHERRIES, WITH PITS

CONFECTIONERS' SUGAR, FOR TOPPING

## DIRECTIONS

1. Preheat the oven to 400°F. Place 6 tablespoons of the butter, ½ cup of the granulated sugar, the flour, salt, vanilla, eggs, and milk in a large mixing bowl and stir until the mixture is well combined and smooth. Set the mixture aside.

2. Grease a 10-inch cast-iron skillet with the remaining butter and put the skillet in the oven to warm up.

3. When the skillet is warm, remove it from the oven, place ½ cup of the granulated sugar in the skillet, and shake to distribute it evenly. Distribute the cherries in the skillet and then pour the batter over them. Sprinkle the remaining granulated sugar on top, place the skillet in the oven, and bake for about 30 minutes, until the custard is golden brown and set in the middle.

4. Remove from the oven, sprinkle the confectioners' sugar on top, and serve immediately, making sure to remind everyone that the cherries still have their pits.

# Grilled Peaches with Bourbon Caramel

YIELD: **6 SERVINGS**

ACTIVE TIME: **20 MINUTES**

TOTAL TIME: **20 MINUTES**

*Dessert doesn't get simpler, or better, than a grilled peach.*

## INGREDIENTS

½ CUP SUGAR

¼ CUP BOURBON,
PLUS 2 TABLESPOONS

¼ CUP HEAVY CREAM, WARMED

1 TABLESPOON UNSALTED BUTTER

1 TEASPOON KOSHER SALT

6 PEACHES, HALVED AND PITTED

1 QUART VANILLA ICE CREAM,
FOR SERVING

## DIRECTIONS

1. Preheat your gas or charcoal grill to 400°F.

2. Place the sugar and ¼ cup of bourbon in a small saucepan and cook over medium heat until the sugar has dissolved. Reduce the heat and add the heavy cream, stirring constantly to incorporate and taking care to mind the splattering caramel. Add the remaining bourbon, the butter, and salt, remove from heat, and pour into a heatproof mixing bowl.

3. When the grill is ready, place the peaches, cut-side down, on the grill and cook until the flesh becomes tender and starts to caramelize, about 5 minutes. Turn the peaches over and cook for another 4 to 5 minutes. Place two or three peach halves in each bowl, drizzle the bourbon caramel over them, and top with vanilla ice cream.

# Plum Galette

YIELD: **4 TO 6 SERVINGS**

ACTIVE TIME: **20 MINUTES**

TOTAL TIME: **1 HOUR**

*The deep red color of the plums against the delicate, golden brown crust makes this galette as appealing to the eye as it is to the taste buds.*

## INGREDIENTS

1 PIECRUST

ALL-PURPOSE FLOUR, FOR DUSTING

3 CUPS PITTED AND SLICED PLUMS

½ CUP SUGAR, PLUS 1 TABLESPOON

JUICE OF ½ LEMON

3 TABLESPOONS CORNSTARCH

1 PINCH KOSHER SALT

2 TABLESPOONS BLACKBERRY JAM

1 EGG, BEATEN

## DIRECTIONS

1. Preheat the oven to 400°F. Place the piecrust on a flour-dusted work surface, roll it out to 9 inches, and place it on a parchment-lined baking sheet.

2. Place the plums, the ½ cup of sugar, lemon juice, cornstarch, and salt in a mixing bowl and stir until the plums are evenly coated.

3. Spread the jam over the crust, making sure to leave 1½ inches of dough around the edge. Spread the filling on top of the jam and fold the uncovered dough over it. Brush the crust with the beaten egg and sprinkle it with the remaining sugar.

4. Put the galette in the oven and bake for 35 to 40 minutes, until the crust is golden brown and the filling is bubbly. Remove from the oven and briefly let cool before serving.

# Raspberry Pie Bars

*The best way to bring the glory of berry season to your loved ones.*

## INGREDIENTS

2 PIECRUSTS

⅔ CUP ALL-PURPOSE FLOUR, PLUS MORE FOR DUSTING

7 CUPS FRESH RASPBERRIES

2 CUPS SUGAR, PLUS MORE TO TASTE

2 TABLESPOONS FRESH LEMON JUICE

1 PINCH KOSHER SALT

1 EGG, BEATEN

## DIRECTIONS

1. Preheat the oven to 350°F and grease a rimmed 15 x 10-inch baking sheet with nonstick cooking spray.

2. Roll out one of the piecrusts on a lightly floured work surface so that it fits the baking sheet. Place it in the pan, press down to ensure that it is even, and prick it with a fork. Roll out the other crust so that it is slightly larger than the baking sheet.

3. Place the raspberries, sugar, flour, lemon juice, and salt in a mixing bowl and stir until well combined. Spread this mixture evenly across the crust in the baking sheet.

4. Place the top crust over the filling and trim any excess. Brush the top crust with the egg and sprinkle additional sugar on top.

5. Place the bars in the oven and bake for about 40 minutes, until golden brown. Remove from the oven and let cool before slicing.

# Dutch Apple Baby

YIELD: **4 SERVINGS**

ACTIVE TIME: **20 MINUTES**

TOTAL TIME: **40 MINUTES**

*The golden-brown burnish of this dessert promises big things, and the powerful trio of apples, cinnamon, and sugar delivers.*

## INGREDIENTS

4 TABLESPOONS UNSALTED BUTTER

2 FIRM AND TART APPLES, CORED, PEELED, AND SLICED

¼ CUP GRANULATED SUGAR, PLUS 3 TABLESPOONS

1 TABLESPOON CINNAMON

¾ CUP ALL-PURPOSE FLOUR

¼ TEASPOON KOSHER SALT

¾ CUP WHOLE MILK

4 EGGS

1 TEASPOON PURE VANILLA EXTRACT

CONFECTIONERS' SUGAR, FOR DUSTING

## DIRECTIONS

1. Preheat the oven to 425°F and place a rack in the middle position. Warm a cast-iron skillet over medium-high heat. Add the butter and apples and cook, while stirring, until the apples start to soften, 3 to 4 minutes. Add the ¼ cup of sugar and the cinnamon and cook for another 3 or 4 minutes. Distribute the apples evenly over the bottom of the skillet and remove from heat.

2. In a large bowl, mix the remaining sugar, flour, and salt together. In a smaller bowl, whisk together the milk, eggs, and vanilla extract. Add the wet mixture to the dry mixture and stir until thoroughly combined. Pour the resulting batter over the apples.

3. Put the skillet in the oven and bake until the pastry is puffy and golden brown, about 20 minutes. Remove the skillet from the oven and let cool for a few minutes. Run a knife along the edge of the skillet to loosen the pastry and then, using oven mitts or pot holders, invert it onto a large plate. Dust with the confectioners' sugar and serve warm.

# Lemon Squares

YIELD: **12 TO 16 SQUARES**

ACTIVE TIME: **15 MINUTES**

TOTAL TIME: **1 HOUR**

*A toothsome lemon custard lets these bars remain light will still satisfying the craving for something sweet.*

## INGREDIENTS

1 STICK UNSALTED BUTTER

⅓ CUP CONFECTIONERS' SUGAR

1 CUP ALL-PURPOSE FLOUR,
PLUS 2 TABLESPOONS

1 PINCH KOSHER SALT

2 LARGE EGGS,
AT ROOM TEMPERATURE

1 CUP GRANULATED SUGAR

⅓ CUP FRESH LEMON JUICE

1 TABLESPOON LEMON ZEST

## DIRECTIONS

1. Preheat the oven to 350°F and grease a square 8-inch cake pan with nonstick cooking spray.

2. Place the butter, ¼ cup of the confectioners' sugar, the 1 cup of flour, and salt in a mixing bowl and stir until the mixture is coarse crumbs. Press mixture into the baking pan and bake for about 20 minutes, until it is set and lightly browned. Remove from the oven and set aside.

3. Place the eggs, granulated sugar, remaining flour, lemon juice, and lemon zest in a mixing bowl and beat until well combined.

4. Pour the custard over the crust and bake for 20 minutes, or until just browned. The custard should still be soft. Let the pan cool on a wire rack before dusting with the remaining confectioners' sugar and cutting into bars.

# Strawberry Rhubarb Crisp

YIELD: **4 SERVINGS**

ACTIVE TIME: **15 MINUTES**

TOTAL TIME: **45 MINUTES**

*The classic sweet-and-sour combo, in a much easier to prepare package.*

## INGREDIENTS

1½ CUPS CHOPPED RHUBARB

1½ CUPS HULLED AND SLICED STRAWBERRIES

2 TABLESPOONS GRANULATED SUGAR

⅓ CUP ALL-PURPOSE FLOUR, PLUS 2 TEASPOONS

4 TABLESPOONS UNSALTED BUTTER, CHILLED AND CUT INTO SMALL PIECES

¼ CUP GENTLY PACKED BROWN SUGAR

¾ CUP OATS

WHIPPED CREAM, FOR SERVING

## DIRECTIONS

1. Preheat the oven to 450°F. Place the rhubarb, strawberries, granulated sugar, and the 2 teaspoons of flour in a bowl and stir to combine. Toss to coat the fruit and then transfer to a baking dish or cast-iron skillet.

2. Place the butter and the brown sugar in a bowl and use a fork to combine. Add the oats and remaining flour and work the mixture until it is a coarse meal. Sprinkle over the fruit mixture in the skillet.

3. Put the skillet in the oven and bake for about 30 minutes, until the topping is golden brown and the filling is bubbling. Serve warm and top each portion with whipped cream.

# Bananas Foster

YIELD: **6 SERVINGS**

ACTIVE TIME: **10 MINUTES**

TOTAL TIME: **10 MINUTES**

*The decadent New Orleans classic is easier than you ever imagined.*

## INGREDIENTS

2 STICKS UNSALTED BUTTER

1 CUP FIRMLY PACKED LIGHT BROWN SUGAR

6 BANANAS, CUT LENGTHWISE AND HALVED

½ CUP DARK RUM

½ CUP HEAVY CREAM

VANILLA ICE CREAM, FOR SERVING

CINNAMON, FOR DUSTING

## DIRECTIONS

1. Place a cast-iron skillet over medium-high heat and add the butter and brown sugar. Once the butter and sugar are melted, add the bananas to the pan and cook until they start to caramelize, about 3 minutes. Spoon the sauce over the bananas as they cook.

2. Remove the pan from heat and add the rum. Using a long match or a wand lighter, carefully ignite the rum. Place the pan back over medium-high heat and shake the pan until the flames have gone out. Add the cream and stir to incorporate.

3. Divide the bananas and sauce between the serving dishes. Top each serving with ice cream and sprinkle cinnamon over everything.

# METRIC CONVERSIONS

| U.S. Measurement | Approximate Metric Liquid Measurement | Approximate Metric Dry Measurement |
|---|---|---|
| 1 teaspoon | 5 ml | 5 g |
| 1 tablespoon or ½ ounce | 15 ml | 14 g |
| 1 ounce or ⅛ cup | 30 ml | 29 g |
| ¼ cup or 2 ounces | 60 ml | 57 g |
| ⅓ cup | 80 ml | 76 g |
| ½ cup or 4 ounces | 120 ml | 113 g |
| ⅔ cup | 160 ml | 151 g |
| ¾ cup or 6 ounces | 180 ml | 170 g |
| 1 cup or 8 ounces or ½ pint | 240 ml | 227 g |
| 1½ cups or 12 ounces | 350 ml | 340 g |
| 2 cups or 1 pint or 16 ounces | 475 ml | 454 g |
| 3 cups or 1½ pints | 700 ml | 680 g |
| 4 cups or 2 pints or 1 quart | 950 ml | 908 g |

# INDEX

## A

almond milk, Sweet Potato Lentils, 95

apples
Curried Chicken Salad, 193
Dutch Apple Baby, 239
Pork & Apple Casserole, 150

arugula
Chicken Paninis with Sun-Dried Tomato Aioli, 213
Chilled Corn Salad, 194
Curried Chicken Salad, 193
Omelet with Arugula, Ricotta, Sun-Dried Tomatoes & Olives, 54

Asparagus with Sunny-Side Eggs & Lemon-Pepper Mayonnaise, Roasted, 149

Avgolemono, 205

avocados
Guacamole, 27
Rice Bowl with Benihana's Ginger Dressing, 190

## B

bacon
Bacon & Zucchini Frittata, 42
BLT with Basil Mayo, 69
Chicken Paninis with Sun-Dried Tomato Aioli, 213
Peanut Butter & Bacon Oats, 45
Skillet Meatloaf with Bacon, 134
Succotash, 50

Bananas Foster, 244

Barley, Sweet & Spicy Roasted, 138

basil
Basil Pesto, 28
BLT with Basil Mayo, 69
Caprese Chicken, 137
Crying Tiger Beef, 172
Marinara Sauce, 31
Panzanella with White Balsamic Vinaigrette, 197
Succotash, 50

Basil Pesto
recipe for, 28
Spaghetti with Zucchini & Pesto, 53

BBQ Sauce, 119

bean sprouts
Pad Thai, 210
Teriyaki Salmon with Vegetables, 81

beans
Chili con Carne, 116
Dry-Fried Beans, 58
Green Bean & Tofu Casserole, 163
Moroccan Lentil Stew, 100
Quinoa & Black Bean Salad, 160
Shredded Chicken with Beans & Rice, 115
Sweet Potato Lentils, 95
Veggie Burgers, 57

beef, Beef Stock, 15

beef and veal
Beef Shawarma, 168
Beef Stew, 99
Carne Asada, 171
Chili con Carne, 116
Coffee & Bourbon Brisket, 119
Crying Tiger Beef, 172
Hungarian Goulash, 103
Kibbeh bil Sanieh, 145
Roast Beef Au Jus with Vegetables, 157
Sichuan Cumin Beef, 175
Skillet Meatloaf with Bacon, 134
Sukiyaki, 74
Thai Beef & Cucumber Salad, 198
Veal Scallopini, 37
Yankee Short Ribs, 127

Beef Stock
Beef Stew, 99
French Onion Soup, 128
recipe for, 15
Roast Beef Au Jus with Vegetables, 157
Veal Scallopini, 37
Yankee Short Ribs, 127

beets
Jerk Chicken with Vegetables, 141
Roast Beef Au Jus with Vegetables, 157

Bigos, 108

black beans
Quinoa & Black Bean Salad, 160
Shredded Chicken with Beans & Rice, 115
Veggie Burgers, 57

Blender Hollandaise, 20

bok choy, Halibut with Braised Vegetables, 106–107

bourbon
Coffee & Bourbon Brisket, 119
Grilled Peaches with Bourbon Caramel, 232

Braised Lamb with Minty Peas, 123

bread
Curried Chicken Salad, 193
French Onion Soup, 128
Ham & Swiss Strata, 186
Mushroom Toast with Whipped Goat Cheese, 89
Panzanella with White Balsamic Vinaigrette, 197
Pizza Dough, 32
Vanilla Bread Pudding, 224

broccoli, Rice Bowl with Benihana's Ginger Dressing, 190

Broccolini, Garlic & Chili, 41

Brussels Sprouts with Hot Honey & Hazelnuts, Roasted, 146

Bulgogi with Musaengchae, 78

bulgur wheat, Kibbeh bil Sanieh, 145

## C

cabbage
Bigos, 108
Halibut with Braised Vegetables, 106–107
See also napa cabbage

Caprese Chicken, 137

Caramel, Grilled Peaches with Bourbon, 232

Carne Asada, 171

carrots
Beef Stew, 99
Braised Lamb with Minty Peas, 123
Hungarian Goulash, 103
Jerk Chicken with Vegetables, 141
Moroccan Lentil Stew, 100
Pork Fried Rice, 201
Rice Bowl with Benihana's Ginger Dressing, 190
Sweet & Spicy Roasted Barley, 138
Thai Beef & Cucumber Salad, 198

cashew milk, Sweet Potato Lentils, 95

casseroles
Chicken & Tomatillo Casserole, 142
Green Bean & Tofu Casserole, 163
Pork & Apple Casserole, 150

Cauliflower & Chickpea Salad, Chili-Dusted, 133

cheddar cheese
  Chicken Paninis with Sun-Dried Tomato Aioli, 213
  Grandma Goodrich's Grits with Shrimp, 46

cheese. *See individual types of cheese*

Cherry Clafoutis, 231

chicken
  Avgolemono, 205
  Caprese Chicken, 137
  Chicken & Coconut with Cucumber Noodles, 209
  Chicken & Sausage Cacciatore, 112
  Chicken & Tomatillo Casserole, 142
  Chicken Kebabs, 167
  Chicken Paninis with Sun-Dried Tomato Aioli, 213
  Chicken Stock, 12
  Chicken Tsukune, 73
  Chicken Vindaloo, 183
  Coconut Curry Chicken with Basmati Rice, 70
  Curried Chicken Salad, 193
  Garden Sesame Noodles, 206
  Jerk Chicken with Vegetables, 141
  Mojo Chicken, 164
  Pad Thai, 210
  Shredded Chicken with Beans & Rice, 115

Chicken Stock
  Avgolemono, 205
  Leftover Turkey Soup, 189
  recipe for, 12
  Shredded Chicken with Beans & Rice, 115
  Tare Sauce, 72

Chickpea Salad, Chili-Dusted Cauliflower &, 133

Chili con Carne, 116

Chili-Dusted Cauliflower & Chickpea Salad, 133

chilies, bird's eye, Thai Red Duck Curry, 90

Chilled Corn Salad, 194

Chinese eggplant, Teriyaki Salmon with Vegetables, 81

Chipotle Sausage & Peppers, 120

chocolate
  Chocolate Chip Cookies, 216
  Chocolate Mousse, 220
  Dark Chocolate & Stout Brownies, 219
  Honey Nut Truffles, 227
  Muddy Buddies, 228

cilantro
  Carne Asada, 171

Chilled Corn Salad, 194
Crying Tiger Beef, 172
Mojo Chicken, 164
Red Snapper with Tomatillo Sauce, 82
Sichuan Cumin Beef, 175

Clafoutis, Cherry, 231

clam juice, Crab & Okra Soup, 49

coconut
  Chicken & Coconut with Cucumber Noodles, 209
  Coconut Curry Chicken with Basmati Rice, 70

coconut milk
  Coconut Curry Chicken with Basmati Rice, 70
  Halibut with Braised Vegetables, 106–107
  Thai Red Duck Curry, 90

Coffee & Bourbon Brisket, 119

Cookies, Chocolate Chip, 216

corn
  Chilled Corn Salad, 194
  Panzanella with White Balsamic Vinaigrette, 197
  Rice Bowl with Benihana's Ginger Dressing, 190
  Succotash, 50
  Veggie Burgers, 57

cotija cheese
  Chicken & Tomatillo Casserole, 142
  Chilled Corn Salad, 194

Crab & Okra Soup, 49

Cranberry Sauce, Pork Loin with Dried, 38

Creamy Curry Kuri Soup, 153

Crying Tiger Beef, 172

cucumbers
  Beef Shawarma, 168
  Chicken & Coconut with Cucumber Noodles, 209
  Garden Sesame Noodles, 206
  Raspberry & Tomato Gazpacho, 176
  Spicy Pickles, 180
  Thai Beef & Cucumber Salad, 198

Cumin Beef, Sichuan, 175

Curried Chicken Salad, 193

**D**

Dal, 96

Dark Chocolate & Stout Brownies, 219

desserts
  Bananas Foster, 244
  Cherry Clafoutis, 231
  Chocolate Chip Cookies, 216
  Chocolate Mousse, 220
  Dark Chocolate & Stout Brownies, 219

Dutch Apple Baby, 239
Grilled Peaches with Bourbon Caramel, 232
Honey Nut Truffles, 227
Lemon Squares, 240
Mille-Feuille, 223
Muddy Buddies, 228
Plum Galette, 235
Raspberry Pie Bars, 236
Strawberry Rhubarb Crisp, 243
Vanilla Bread Pudding, 224

dips
  Guacamole, 27
  Roasted Tomato Salsa, 23
  Salsa Verde, 24

dressings
  Ginger Dressing, 190
  White Balsamic Vinaigrette, 197

Dry Rub
  Coffee & Bourbon Brisket, 119
  recipe for, 118

Duck Curry, Thai Red, 90

Dutch Apple Baby, 239

**E**

edamame
  Rice Bowl with Benihana's Ginger Dressing, 190
  Succotash, 50

eggplant
  Halibut with Braised Vegetables, 106–107
  Ratatouille, 104
  Teriyaki Salmon with Vegetables, 81

eggs
  Avgolemono, 205
  Bacon & Zucchini Frittata, 42
  Green Shakshuka, 65
  Ham & Swiss Strata, 186
  Omelet with Arugula, Ricotta, Sun-Dried Tomatoes & Olives, 54
  Pad Thai, 210
  Peanut Butter & Bacon Oats, 45
  Pork Fried Rice, 201
  Roasted Asparagus with Sunny-Side Eggs & Lemon-Pepper Mayonnaise, 149

Emmental cheese, French Onion Soup, 128

**F**

feta cheese, Chilled Corn Salad, 194

fish
  Fish Stock, 16
  Halibut with Braised Vegetables, 106–107

Red Snapper with Tomatillo Sauce, 82
Teriyaki Salmon with Vegetables, 81
*See also* seafood
fish sauce
Coconut Curry Chicken with Basmati Rice, 70
Thai Red Duck Curry, 90
Fish Stock
Halibut with Braised Vegetables, 106–107
recipe for, 16
Five-Spice Turkey Breast, 154
French Onion Soup, 128

## G

Galette, Plum, 235
Garden Sesame Noodles, 206
garlic
Garlic & Chili Broccolini, 41
Garlic Shrimp, 85
Mojo Chicken, 164
Gazpacho, Raspberry & Tomato, 176
ginger, fresh
Bulgogi with Musaengchae, 78
Chicken & Coconut with Cucumber Noodles, 209
Chicken Vindaloo, 183
Coconut Curry Chicken with Basmati Rice, 70
Coffee & Bourbon Brisket, 119
Garden Sesame Noodles, 206
Halibut with Braised Vegetables, 106–107
Jerk Chicken with Vegetables, 141
Lamb & Peas Curry, 61
Moroccan Lentil Stew, 100
Pork Fried Rice, 201
Rogan Josh, 124
Saag Aloo, 66
Teriyaki Salmon with Vegetables, 81
goat cheese
Bacon & Zucchini Frittata, 42
Mushroom Toast with Whipped Goat Cheese, 89
gochujang (Korean chili paste), Bulgogi with Musaengchae, 78
Grandma Goodrich's Grits with Shrimp, 46
green beans
Dry-Fried Beans, 58
Green Bean & Tofu Casserole, 163
Green Shakshuka, 65
Grilled Peaches with Bourbon Caramel, 232
Grits with Shrimp, Grandma Goodrich's, 46

Gruyère cheese, French Onion Soup, 128
Guacamole
recipe for, 27
Red Snapper with Tomatillo Sauce, 82
Veggie Burgers, 57

## H

Halibut with Braised Vegetables, 106–107
Ham & Swiss Strata, 186
Hash, Lamb & Sweet Potato, 202
Hazelnuts, Roasted Brussels Sprouts with Hot Honey &, 146
honey
Green Bean & Tofu Casserole, 163
Honey Nut Truffles, 227
Hot Honey, 146
Roasted Brussels Sprouts with Hot Honey & Hazelnuts, 146
horseradish, Spicy Tonkatsu, 77
Hungarian Goulash, 103

## J

Jerk Chicken with Vegetables, 141

## K

kale, Halibut with Braised Vegetables, 106–107
Kibbeh bil Sanieh, 145
kielbasa
Bigos, 108
Chipotle Sausage & Peppers, 120
*See also* sausage
Kimchi, 179
Kuri Soup, Creamy Curry, 153

## L

lamb
Braised Lamb with Minty Peas, 123
Lamb & Pea Curry, 61
Lamb & Sweet Potato Hash, 202
Rogan Josh, 124
leeks, Beef Stew, 99
Leftover Turkey Soup, 189
leftovers
Avgolemono, 205
Chicken & Coconut with Cucumber Noodles, 209
Chicken Paninis with Sun-Dried Tomato Aioli, 213
Chilled Corn Salad, 194
Curried Chicken Salad, 193
Garden Sesame Noodles, 206
Ham & Swiss Strata, 186

Lamb & Sweet Potato Hash, 202
Leftover Turkey Soup, 189
Pad Thai, 210
Panzanella with White Balsamic Vinaigrette, 197
Pork Fried Rice, 201
Rice Bowl with Benihana's Ginger Dressing, 190
Thai Beef & Cucumber Salad, 198
Lemon Squares, 240
Lemon-Pepper Mayonnaise, Roasted Asparagus with Sunny-Side Eggs &, 149
lentils
Moroccan Lentil Stew, 100
Sweet Potato Lentils, 95
lettuce, Chilled Corn Salad, 194
limes, Thai Red Duck Curry, 90

## M

maple syrup, Sweet Potato Lentils, 95
marinades, recipes with
Beef Shawarma, 168
Carne Asada, 171
Chicken Kebabs, 167
Chicken Vindaloo, 183
Crying Tiger Beef, 172
Green Bean & Tofu Casserole, 163
Kimchi, 179
Mojo Chicken, 164
Quinoa & Black Bean Salad, 160
Raspberry & Tomato Gazpacho, 176
Sichuan Cumin Beef, 175
Marinara Sauce, 31
mayonnaise
Chicken Paninis with Sun-Dried Tomato Aioli, 213
Roasted Asparagus with Sunny-Side Eggs & Lemon-Pepper Mayonnaise, 149
Meatloaf with Bacon, Skillet, 134
Mille-Feuille, 223
mint
Beef Shawarma, 168
Braised Lamb with Minty Peas, 123
Crying Tiger Beef, 172
Mojo Chicken, 164
Moroccan Lentil Stew, 100
Mousse, Chocolate, 220
mozzarella cheese, Caprese Chicken, 137
Muddy Buddies, 228
Musaengchae, Bulgogi with, 78
mushrooms
Green Bean & Tofu Casserole, 163
Mushroom Toast with Whipped Goat

Cheese, 89

Spinach & Mushroom Quinoa, 111

Succotash, 50

Sukiyaki, 74

**N**

napa cabbage

Kimchi, 179

Sukiyaki, 74

*See also* cabbage

nectarine, Coffee & Bourbon Brisket, 119

noodles. See pasta and noodles

**O**

Oats, Peanut Butter & Bacon, 45

Okra Soup, Crab &, 49

Olives, Omelet with Arugula, Ricotta, Sun-Dried Tomatoes &, 54

Omelet with Arugula, Ricotta, Sun-Dried Tomatoes & Olives, 54

onions

Beef Shawarma, 168

Bigos, 108

French Onion Soup, 128

Lamb & Sweet Potato Hash, 202

Panzanella with White Balsamic Vinaigrette, 197

Rogan Josh, 124

Yankee Short Ribs, 127

orzo, Avgolemono, 205

oven recipes

Caprese Chicken, 137

Chicken & Tomatillo Casserole, 142

Chili-Dusted Cauliflower & Chickpea Salad, 133

Creamy Curry Kuri Soup, 153

Five-Spice Turkey Breast, 154

Jerk Chicken with Vegetables, 141

Kibbeh bil Sanieh, 145

Pork & Apple Casserole, 150

Roasted Asparagus with Sunny-Side Eggs & Lemon-Pepper Mayonnaise, 149

Roasted Brussels Sprouts with Hot Honey & Hazelnuts, 146

Skillet Meatloaf with Bacon, 134

Sweet & Spicy Roasted Barley, 138

**P**

Pad Thai, 210

Panzanella with White Balsamic Vinaigrette, 197

Parmesan cheese

Basil Pesto, 28

Roasted Asparagus with Sunny-Side Eggs & Lemon-Pepper Mayonnaise, 149

Roasted Brussels Sprouts with Hot Honey & Hazelnuts, 146

parsnips, Roast Beef Au Jus with Vegetables, 157

pasta and noodles

Avgolemono, 205

Bigos, 108

Chicken & Coconut with Cucumber Noodles, 209

Garden Sesame Noodles, 206

Hungarian Goulash, 103

Leftover Turkey Soup, 189

Pad Thai, 210

Spaghetti with Zucchini & Pesto, 53

Sukiyaki, 74

Thai Beef & Cucumber Salad, 198

Pastry Cream

Mille-Feuille, 223

recipe for, 222

peaches

Coffee & Bourbon Brisket, 119

Grilled Peaches with Bourbon Caramel, 232

peanut butter

Honey Nut Truffles, 227

Muddy Buddies, 228

Peanut Butter & Bacon Oats, 45

peanuts

Chicken & Coconut with Cucumber Noodles, 209

Crab & Okra Soup, 49

Garden Sesame Noodles, 206

Pad Thai, 210

peas

Braised Lamb with Minty Peas, 123

Dal, 96

Garden Sesame Noodles, 206

Lamb & Pea Curry, 61

Pork Fried Rice, 201

Spring Pea Soup with Lemon Ricotta, 86

pecans, Curried Chicken Salad, 193

pecorino sardo cheese, Basil Pesto, 28

peppers, hot

Carne Asada, 171

Chicken & Tomatillo Casserole, 142

Chili con Carne, 116

Chili-Dusted Cauliflower & Chickpea Salad, 133

Chilled Corn Salad, 194

Chipotle Sausage & Peppers, 120

Crab & Okra Soup, 49

Guacamole, 27

Halibut with Braised Vegetables, 106–107

Jerk Chicken with Vegetables, 141

Kibbeh bil Sanieh, 145

Lamb & Sweet Potato Hash, 202

Mojo Chicken, 164

Quinoa & Black Bean Salad, 160

Red Snapper with Tomatillo Sauce, 82

Roast Beef Au Jus with Vegetables, 157

Roasted Tomato Salsa, 23

Salsa Verde, 24

Shredded Chicken with Beans & Rice, 115

Sichuan Cumin Beef, 175

Spicy Pickles, 180

Sweet & Spicy Roasted Barley, 138

peppers, sweet

Chicken & Sausage Cacciatore, 112

Chili con Carne, 116

Chipotle Sausage & Peppers, 120

Coconut Curry Chicken with Basmati Rice, 70

Crab & Okra Soup, 49

Curried Chicken Salad, 193

Garden Sesame Noodles, 206

Halibut with Braised Vegetables, 106–107

Hungarian Goulash, 103

Quinoa & Black Bean Salad, 160

Raspberry & Tomato Gazpacho, 176

Ratatouille, 104

Spicy Pickles, 180

Spinach & Mushroom Quinoa, 111

Succotash, 50

Teriyaki Salmon with Vegetables, 81

Veggie Burgers, 57

pesto

Basil Pesto, 28

Spaghetti with Zucchini & Pesto, 53

Pickles, Spicy, 180

pine nuts, Kibbeh bil Sanieh, 145

pineapple, Thai Red Duck Curry, 90

Pizza Dough, 32

Plum Galette, 235

pork

Bulgogi with Musaengchae, 78

Dry-Fried Beans, 58

Pork & Apple Casserole, 150

Pork Fried Rice, 201

Pork Loin with Dried Cranberry Sauce, 38

Skillet Meatloaf with Bacon, 134

Spicy Tonkatsu, 77

*See also* bacon; ham; sausage

potatoes

Beef Stew, 99

Jerk Chicken with Vegetables, 141
Saag Aloo, 66
Yankee Short Ribs, 127

## Q

quick dishes
  Bacon & Zucchini Frittata, 42
  BLT with Basil Mayo, 69
  Bulgogi with Musaengchae, 78
  Chicken Tsukune, 73
  Coconut Curry Chicken with Basmati Rice, 70
  Crab & Okra Soup, 49
  Dry-Fried Beans, 58
  Garlic & Chili Broccolini, 41
  Garlic Shrimp, 85
  Grandma Goodrich's Grits with Shrimp, 46
  Green Shakshuka, 65
  Lamb & Pea Curry, 61
  Mushroom Toast with Whipped Goat Cheese, 89
  Omelet with Arugula, Ricotta, Sun-Dried Tomatoes & Olives, 54
  Peanut Butter & Bacon Oats, 45
  Pork Loin with Dried Cranberry Sauce, 38
  Red Snapper with Tomatillo Sauce, 82
  Saag Aloo, 66
  Spaghetti with Zucchini & Pesto, 53
  Spicy Tonkatsu, 77
  Spring Pea Soup with Lemon Ricotta, 86
  Succotash, 50
  Sukiyaki, 74
  Teriyaki Salmon with Vegetables, 81
  Thai Red Duck Curry, 90
  Tofu Tacos, 62
  Veal Scallopini, 37
  Veggie Burgers, 57
quinoa
  Quinoa & Black Bean Salad, 160
  Spinach & Mushroom Quinoa, 111

## R

raspberries
  Mille-Feuille, 223
  Raspberry & Tomato Gazpacho, 176
  Raspberry Pie Bars, 236
Ratatouille, 104
Red Snapper with Tomatillo Sauce, 82
Rhubarb Crisp, Strawberry, 243
rice
  Chicken & Sausage Cacciatore, 112
  Coconut Curry Chicken with Basmati

Rice, 70
Pork Fried Rice, 201
Rice Bowl with Benihana's Ginger Dressing, 190
Shredded Chicken with Beans & Rice, 115
Thai Red Duck Curry, 90
ricotta
  Omelet with Arugula, Ricotta, Sun-Dried Tomatoes & Olives, 54
  Spring Pea Soup with Lemon Ricotta, 86
Roast Beef Au Jus with Vegetables, 157
Roasted Asparagus with Sunny-Side Eggs & Lemon-Pepper Mayonnaise, 149
Roasted Brussels Sprouts with Hot Honey & Hazelnuts, 146
Roasted Tomato Salsa, 23
Rogan Josh, 124
rum, Bananas Foster, 244

## S

Saag Aloo, 66
salads
  Chili-Dusted Cauliflower & Chickpea Salad, 133
  Chilled Corn Salad, 194
  Curried Chicken Salad, 193
  Quinoa & Black Bean Salad, 160
  Thai Beef & Cucumber Salad, 198
Salmon with Vegetables, Teriyaki, 81
salsa
  Chicken & Tomatillo Casserole, 142
  Quinoa & Black Bean Salad, 160
  Roasted Tomato Salsa, 23
  Salsa Verde, 24
sandwiches
  BLT with Basil Mayo, 69
  Chicken Paninis with Sun-Dried Tomato Aioli, 213
  Veggie Burgers, 57
sauces
  Basil Pesto, 28
  Blender Hollandaise, 20
  Marinara Sauce, 31
sausage
  Bigos, 108
  Chicken & Sausage Cacciatore, 112
  Chipotle Sausage & Peppers, 120
scallions
  Kimchi, 179
  Sukiyaki, 74
seafood
  Crab & Okra Soup, 49
  Garlic Shrimp, 85

Grandma Goodrich's Grits with Shrimp, 46
Halibut with Braised Vegetables, 106–107
Red Snapper with Tomatillo Sauce, 82
Teriyaki Salmon with Vegetables, 81
Sesame Noodles, Garden, 206
shallots, Spring Pea Soup with Lemon Ricotta, 86
Shredded Chicken with Beans & Rice, 115
shrimp
  Garlic Shrimp, 85
  Grandma Goodrich's Grits with Shrimp, 46
Sichuan Cumin Beef, 175
Skillet Meatloaf with Bacon, 134
slow-cooking recipes
  Beef Stew, 99
  Bigos, 108
  Braised Lamb with Minty Peas, 123
  Chicken & Sausage Cacciatore, 112
  Chili con Carne, 116
  Chipotle Sausage & Peppers, 120
  Coffee & Bourbon Brisket, 119
  Dal, 96
  French Onion Soup, 128
  Halibut with Braised Vegetables, 106–107
  Hungarian Goulash, 103
  Moroccan Lentil Stew, 100
  Ratatouille, 104
  Rogan Josh, 124
  Shredded Chicken with Beans & Rice, 115
  Spinach & Mushroom Quinoa, 111
  Sweet Potato Lentils, 95
  Yankee Short Ribs, 127
soups and stews
  Beef Stew, 99
  Beef Stock, 15
  Chicken Stock, 12
  Chili con Carne, 116
  Crab & Okra Soup, 49
  Creamy Curry Kuri Soup, 153
  Fish Stock, 16
  French Onion Soup, 128
  Hungarian Goulash, 103
  Leftover Turkey Soup, 189
  Moroccan Lentil Stew, 100
  Raspberry & Tomato Gazpacho, 176
  Spring Pea Soup with Lemon Ricotta, 86
  Vegetable Stock, 19
Spaghetti with Zucchini & Pesto, 53
Spicy Pickles, 180

Spicy Tonkatsu, 77
spinach
  Bacon & Zucchini Frittata, 42
  Crab & Okra Soup, 49
  Green Shakshuka, 65
  Ham & Swiss Strata, 186
  Quinoa & Black Bean Salad, 160
  Saag Aloo, 66
  Spinach & Mushroom Quinoa, 111
  Sukiyaki, 74
Spring Pea Soup with Lemon Ricotta, 86
squash, Creamy Curry Kuri Soup, 153
staples
  Basil Pesto, 28
  Beef Stock, 15
  Blender Hollandaise, 20
  Chicken Stock, 12
  Fish Stock, 16
  Guacamole, 27
  Marinara Sauce, 31
  Pizza Dough, 32
  Roasted Tomato Salsa, 23
  Salsa Verde, 24
  Vegetable Stock, 19
Stout Brownies, Dark Chocolate &, 219
Strawberry Rhubarb Crisp, 243
Succotash, 50
sun-dried tomatoes
  Chicken Paninis with Sun-Dried Tomato Aioli, 213
  Omelet with Arugula, Ricotta, Sun-Dried Tomatoes & Olives, 54
sunflower seeds, Mushroom Toast with Whipped Goat Cheese, 89
Sweet & Spicy Roasted Barley, 138
sweet potatoes
  Lamb & Sweet Potato Hash, 202
  Sweet Potato Lentils, 95
Swiss cheese, Ham & Swiss Strata, 186

**T**
Tacos, Tofu, 62
Tare Sauce
  Chicken Tsukune, 73
  recipe for, 72
Teriyaki Salmon with Vegetables, 81
Thai Beef & Cucumber Salad, 198
Thai Red Duck Curry, 90
Toasted Rice Powder
  Crying Tiger Beef, 172
  recipe for, 173
tofu
  Green Bean & Tofu Casserole, 163
  Rice Bowl with Benihana's Ginger

Dressing, 190
  Sukiyaki, 74
  Tofu Tacos, 62
tomatillos
  Chicken & Tomatillo Casserole, 142
  Green Shakshuka, 65
  Quinoa & Black Bean Salad, 160
  Red Snapper with Tomatillo Sauce, 82
  Salsa Verde, 24
tomatoes
  Beef Shawarma, 168
  BLT with Basil Mayo, 69
  Caprese Chicken, 137
  Chicken & Sausage Cacciatore, 112
  Chicken & Tomatillo Casserole, 142
  Chicken Paninis with Sun-Dried Tomato Aioli, 213
  Chicken Vindaloo, 183
  Chili con Carne, 116
  Chipotle Sausage & Peppers, 120
  Crying Tiger Beef, 172
  Lamb & Pea Curry, 61
  Marinara Sauce, 31
  Omelet with Arugula, Ricotta, Sun-Dried Tomatoes & Olives, 54
  Panzanella with White Balsamic Vinaigrette, 197
  Raspberry & Tomato Gazpacho, 176
  Ratatouille, 104
  Roasted Tomato Salsa, 23
  Rogan Josh, 124
  Shredded Chicken with Beans & Rice, 115
  Thai Red Duck Curry, 90
  Tomato Concasse, 27
tortillas
  Carne Asada, 171
  Chicken & Tomatillo Casserole, 142
turkey
  Five-Spice Turkey Breast, 154
  Leftover Turkey Soup, 189
turnips, Jerk Chicken with Vegetables, 141

**V**
Vanilla Bread Pudding, 224
Veal Scallopini, 37. See also beef and veal
Vegetable Stock
  Crab & Okra Soup, 49
  Moroccan Lentil Stew, 100
  recipe for, 19
  Spinach & Mushroom Quinoa, 111

**W**

walnuts, Basil Pesto, 28
wasabi paste, Spicy Tonkatsu, 77
White Balsamic Vinaigrette, Panzanella, 197

**Y**
Yankee Short Ribs, 127
yogurt
  Beef Shawarma, 168
  Chicken Kebabs, 167
  Lamb & Pea Curry, 61
  Rogan Josh, 124
  Saag Aloo, 66

**Z**
zucchini
  Bacon & Zucchini Frittata, 42
  Ratatouille, 104
  Spaghetti with Zucchini & Pesto, 53

# ABOUT CIDER MILL PRESS
## BOOK PUBLISHERS

---

Good ideas ripen with time. From seed to harvest, Cider Mill Press brings fine reading, information, and entertainment together between the covers of its creatively crafted books. Our Cider Mill bears fruit twice a year, publishing a new crop of titles each spring and fall.

"Where Good Books Are Ready for Press"

Visit us online at
www.cidermillpress.com
or write to us at
PO Box 454
12 Spring St.
Kennebunkport, Maine 04046